COMPLETE WORKS

RECENT RESEARCHES IN THE MUSIC OF THE MIDDLE AGES AND EARLY RENAISSANCE

Margaret Bent, General editor

A-R Editions, Inc., publishes six quarterly series—

Recent Researches in the Music of the Middle Ages and Early Renaissance
Margaret Bent, general editor

Recent Researches in the Music of the Renaissance
James Haar, general editor

Recent Researches in the Music of the Baroque Era
Robert L. Marshall, general editor

Recent Researches in the Music of the Classical Era
Eugene K. Wolf, general editor

Recent Researches in the Music of the Nineteenth and Early Twentieth Centuries
Rufus Hallmark, general editor

Recent Researches in American Music
H. Wiley Hitchcock, general editor—

which make public music that is being brought to light
in the course of current musicological research.

Each volume in the *Recent Researches* is devoted
to works by a single composer or to a single genre of composition,
chosen because of its potential interest to scholars and performers,
and prepared for publication according to the standards that govern
the making of all reliable historical editions.

Subscribers to this series, as well as patrons of subscribing institutions,
are invited to apply for information about the "Copyright-Sharing Policy"
of A-R Editions, Inc., under which the contents of this volume
may be reproduced free of charge for study or performance.

Correspondence should be addressed:

A-R EDITIONS, INC.
315 West Gorham Street
Madison, Wisconsin 53703

RECENT RESEARCHES IN THE MUSIC OF THE MIDDLE AGES
AND EARLY RENAISSANCE • VOLUME XV

Johannes Cornago

COMPLETE WORKS

Edited by Rebecca L. Gerber

A-R EDITIONS, INC. • MADISON

© 1984 by A-R Editions, Inc.
All rights reserved
Printed in the United States of America

Library of Congress Cataloging in Publication Data:

Cornago, Juan, 15th cent.
   [Vocal music]
   Complete works.

   (Recent researches in the music of the Middle Ages
and early Renaissance, ISSN 0362-3572 ; v. 15)
   The 2nd work is a motet.
   For 3–4 voices.
   "The lower voices are usually performed by
instruments"—Pref.
   Italian, Latin, or Spanish words.
   Contents: The sacred music: Missa Ayo visto ; Patres
nostri peccaverunt   The secular music: ¿Donde estas
que non te veo? ; Gentil dama non se gana ; [etc.]
   1. Masses.   2. Motets.   3. Part-songs.   I. Gerber,
Rebecca L.   II. Series.
M2.R2383   vol. 15   [M3]   83-15913
ISBN 0-89579-193-5

Contents

Preface	vii
Johannes Cornago	vii
The Music	viii
Sources	xiii
Editorial Methods and Performance Practice	xv
Critical Notes and Texts and Translations	xvi
Acknowledgments	xxix
Notes	xxix

The Sacred Music

Missa "Ayo visto"	1
Patres nostri peccaverunt	36

The Secular Music

¿Donde estas que non te veo?	38
Gentil dama non se gana	40
Moro perche non day fede	41
Morte o merce	43
Non gusto del male estranio	45
Porque mas sin duda creas	46
Pues que Dios te fizo tal	49
¿Qu'es mi vida preguntays?	51
Segun las penas me days	53
Yerra con poco saber	56

Appendix:
Alternate Versions and Double Attributions

Gentil dama non se gana		61
Morthe merce		63
Pues que Dios te fiso tal		64
Pues que Dios te fiso tal	[Cornago]	67
¿Qu'es mi vida preguntays?	Cornago-Ockeghem	69
Señora, qual soy venido	Cornago-Triana	72

Preface

Johannes Cornago

Continental music in the fifteenth century was dominated by Franco-Flemish musicians. Even in the Italian courts, where the cultivation of music flourished, musicians were imported from the north to fill the chapels of the peninsula. In the first half of the century, native Italian and Spanish musicians thrived only at the Aragonese court of Naples. Humanism and the arts prospered enormously under the reign of Alfonso I, king of Naples and Sicily from 1433 until his death in 1458 and king of Aragon from 1416 to 1458 (where he is known as Alfonso V). Alfonso, known in his own time as "the magnanimous," was patron of the humanists Lorenzo Valla, Panormita, and Pontano at Naples. A humanist himself, Alfonso had Aristotle's *Natural History* translated into Spanish and customarily listened to the works of Virgil at dinner. He provided an education for many members of his court at his own expense and sent numerous young men to Rome and Paris to learn grammar, fine arts, and other disciplines.[1]

Alfonso's court at Naples was undoubtedly the most splendid on the peninsula. Although other courts employed only a few musicians at any time before about 1470, Naples already employed more than twenty singers during the 1440s and 1450s.[2] Alfonso's chapels at Naples and Barcelona had been modeled after that of Rome in the 1420s to 1440s.[3] In the second half of the century, however, courts such as Milan, Ferrara, and Rome modeled their chapels on that of Naples.

The court of Naples was cosmopolitan, and foreign musicians were invited to it with promises of employment and gifts. Nevertheless, Alfonso seems to have favored musicians from his native land of Spain. Among his Spanish musicians was Johannes Cornago, one of the earliest Spanish Renaissance composers whose sacred and secular music has survived and for whom biographical material exists. Cornago is first mentioned in connection with the court of Naples in a document dated October 12, 1455, and sent to Rome by Alfonso.[4] It reveals that Cornago was a Franciscan who was residing in Rome in the king's service and receiving extremely generous payments of 300 ducats annually. The purpose of Cornago's stay in Rome is unknown, but it is likely that he, like other Neapolitan courtiers, had been sent there to pursue his education. Also in 1455, Alfonso had sent "a magnificent array of Spanish and Neapolitan nobles and clergy to represent him at the papal coronation to perform homage to Calixtus in his name."[5] Undoubtedly, this delegation included an entourage of musicians, and it is quite possible that Cornago was one of them. Our next actual record of Cornago shows that salary payments of 150 ducats were made to him on September 15, 1456, and January 8, 1457, confirming his annual salary of 300 ducats.[6] Judging from his extraordinary salary, one may conclude that Cornago was already a composer of considerable stature by this time.

Alfonso was succeeded on his death in 1458 by his illegitimate son Ferdinand (1458–1494), who developed a more truly Italian-Neapolitan culture for his court. The number of Italian and Franco-Flemish musicians increased significantly during Ferdinand's reign and included the renowned fifteenth-century theorist Johannes Tinctoris. As a result, many of the Spanish musicians who had been in the service of Alfonso returned to Spain. Cornago, however, remained in Naples for a considerable time under Ferdinand. In 1466, he is mentioned as chief almoner (i.e., dispenser of royal charity) to Ferdinand.[7] On April 3, 1466, Cornago received ten ducats and a tarì to pay for the cost of altering garments in the royal wardrobe which Ferdinand was to give to thirty-four poor persons on Maundy Thursday. On the same day, he received twenty-five ducats to distribute as alms on Good Friday during the king's adoration of the cross. What we know about Cornago's duties other than as composer and musician at the court is consistent with our knowledge of the role of the composer and cleric in both sacred and secular courts throughout the fifteenth century.[8]

By not later than 1475, Cornago had returned to Spain as a singer in the service of Ferdinand the Catholic, nephew of Alfonso and future king of Aragon.[9] It is quite likely, however, that Cornago's return to Spain was not much before 1475. Isabel married Ferdinand in 1469 and became queen of Castile in 1474. Ferdinand, however, did not become king of Aragon until 1479, when the two kingdoms were united. Possibly, Cornago returned to Spain at a time when the two were forming magnificent chapels in honor of the crowning of Isabel. After 1475, there are no known records of Cornago.

The Music

Although we know a great deal about the presence of Spanish musicians at Naples before the middle of the fifteenth century, no polyphonic compositions by Spaniards have survived. The earliest such datable Spanish piece is the anonymous *Versos fechos en loor del Condestable* from 1466.[10] Before this time, however, Spanish music was highly praised by, among others, the renowned poet, the Marqués de Santillana. In a letter of 1441, Santillana explained that he preferred Spanish poetry above all, because, even though the French are masters of form (an artificial art), the Spanish are masters of imagination and of knowing how to sing their poetry to beautiful sounds.[11] Possibly Santillana was speaking of polyphonic songs in the style of Cornago's generation. Only a handful of mid-fifteenth-century Spanish composers besides Cornago are known to us; they include Pietro Oriola, Fernand Pérez de Medina, Bernard Ycart, and Juan Fernández de Madrid. Of these, only Oriola and Cornago are cited in the archival records in the 1440s and 1450s; there are no records of the other composers until the 1470s.

Few sacred compositions by these composers survive; most of them are motets. Besides the *Missa "Ayo visto"* of Cornago, only one movement of a Mass, a Gloria, by Fernández de Madrid is known to us.[12] It is based on the introit "Gaudeamus omnes in Domino." Unfortunately, we have no way of knowing whether Madrid's *cantus firmus* Gloria is a part of a cyclic mass. Cornago's Mass, then, is historically and musically significant for the history of the *cantus firmus* Mass and especially for that of Spanish sacred music.[13]

The Sacred Music

The *Missa "Ayo visto"* is a cyclic mass based on a secular *cantus firmus*. Along with Dufay's *Missa "Se la face ay pale"*[14] and Frye's now fragmentary *Missa "So ys emprentid,"*[15] it is among the earliest Masses based on a secular tune. The song "Ayo visto" is apparently a popular Sicilian song. The refrain of the text can be found beneath the tenor of the *Qui tollis* and *Et resurrexit* in the Mass as preserved in Trent, Castello del Buon Consiglio, MS 88, and reads as follows:

Ayo visto lo mappamundi
et la carta di navigare
ma chichilia me pare
la la più bella, la più bella de questo mundo.

(I have seen the globe of the world and mariner's chart, but Sicily seems to me the most beautiful in this world.)[16]

According to Alessandro D'Ancona, there are references to this song in two collections of *laude*: Florence, Biblioteca Nazionale, Cod. Magl. VII, 744 (with only the incipit "Aggio visto l'appamondo") and Munich, Bayerische Staatsbibliothek, Cod. Ital. 230 as follows:[17]

Aggio visto lo appamondo
e la carta da navicare
ma Cicilia pure mi pare
la più bella isola del mondo.

The Munich manuscript clarifies the obvious errors in the Trent version. Although "ayo" may be a dialectic form of "aggio," the word "chichilia" is clearly the result of a German scribe interpreting into German phonetics the Italian "Cicilia".[18] The last two lines of the Munich version, then, translate "but Sicily still seems to me the most beautiful island in the world."

In the collection of spiritual *laude* by Feo Belcari, the *lauda* "Haggio visto il cieco mondo" (No. CLXV) is printed with the following rubric: "Cantasi come- 'Aggio visto l'ammappamondo' e come 'Purità Dio ti mantegna.' "[19] ("Sung as 'I have seen the globe of the world' and as 'God maintains you in purity.' ") The *lauda*, "Haggio visto," is in the form of a *barzelletta*, and it has the same rhyme scheme as that of our song "Ayo visto." These factors suggest that the song may also be in the form of a *barzelletta*. Unfortunately, this cannot be confirmed since only the *ripresa* of the original song has survived.

The music of the song has not been preserved except in the statements of the *cantus firmus* of Cornago's Mass. Of the ten *cantus firmus* repetitions, as many as five contain no melodic variants except for repetitions of untied notes. These five statements are in the *Qui tollis, Cum sancto, Patrem omnipotentem, Et resurrexit,* and *Et expecto* of the Mass. Three sections, the *Et in terra,* Sanctus, and Osanna II, contain very few pitch variants, none of which are consistently used or else which serve simply as cadential elaborations. Finally, two sections are melodically elaborated throughout the statement so that the *cantus firmus* is not always clearly recognizable; these are the Kyrie I and the Agnus I and III.

Neither the duet sections in the Mass, *Pleni sunt*, Benedictus, and Agnus II, nor, for that matter, the three-voiced Christe and Kyrie II contain any *cantus firmus* material except for a few resemblances of motivic ideas from the song.

Although the original rhythmic values of the song cannot be determined with complete accuracy from the *cantus firmus*, many rhythmic patterns occur so consistently that they cannot be ignored. It is not likely that they are a result of Cornago's compositional procedures, since the rhythms and phrases of the melody appear to be constructed to fit the text of the song. Two of the *cantus firmus* statements are nearly identical melodically and rhythmically; they occur in the final statements of the Gloria and Credo.[20] These sections also contain the shortest note values of the *cantus firmus* statements in the Mass, values that correspond rhythmically to those in most contemporaneous songs. Such statements in short note values of a virtually unornamented *cantus firmus* are commonly found at these points in a large number of other mid-fifteenth-century *cantus firmus* Masses, e.g., in the "Se la face ay pale" and "L'homme armé" Masses of Dufay and in Ockeghem's "L'homme armé" Mass (Gloria only). Below (Ex. 1) is a reconstruction of the original song with only the *ripresa* set to the music, as it might have appeared in a Petrucci print of *frottole* nearly a half-century later.[21] The text in the example below preserves the dialectic Italian spellings, while the obvious grammatical mistakes and omissions made by the German scribe of Trent 88 have been corrected. Reconstruction of the *lauda* "Haggio visto" (Ex. 2), which follows the incomplete song "Ayo visto" shows the form of the *barzelletta* as it would have been performed in its entirety. (The text is taken from Belcari, *Laude spirituali*, p. 75 and translated by William Prizer.)

Example 1

Example 2

I have seen the blind world and its false delight; its every pleasure seems to me full of bitterness and heavy weight. See the body and its beauty, lost through a brief illness; see the rich man in his high place descend so quickly the stairs. Among those in the magisterial seat, see the worthy, wise man pulled down and villified. I have seen the blind world and its false delight.

Numerous attempts have been made to date the Mass, or more specifically the song itself, on the basis of accounts of tapestries or maps of the world to which this song could have referred.[22] But clearly the song, despite its initial line, is not so much a song about maps as it is about Sicily's beauty. Thus it may be more likely that it was simply a popular Sicilian song that made its way to Naples during Alfonso's conquests of both Naples and Sicily.

An inscription above the Mass in Trent 88 (Trent, Castello del Buon Consiglio, MS 88) indicates in Italianate Latin that it was used in feasts of the Virgin Mary: "Frater Johannes Cornago. La missa de la mapamundi apud Neapolim et la missa de nostra dona Sancta Maria."[23] The connection of the Virgin Mary with navigators had been a commonplace of medieval thought. This is amply demonstrated by the hymn "Ave maris stella" (sung at all vespers of the Virgin), by the "Alma redemptoris mater" of Hermanus Contractus (1013–1054), and by a larger body of sequences (among them, the well-known Victorine sequence "Ave virgo singularis"), all of which refer to Mary as the star of the sea. That Columbus christened his flagship the *Santa Maria* is probably no coincidence.

The most striking characteristic of Cornago's Mass is its apparent stylistic similarity to English music. Although we have no evidence of any English composers at the court of Naples at this time, and although the number of English musicians working on the continent in the fifteenth century was relatively small, it is a well-known fact that from the early decades of the fifteenth century to about the third quarter of the century, English music was widely circulated and admired throughout Europe, and particularly in Italy. Most of the sources of English music are, in fact, north Italian and Neapolitan.

Stylistically, the Mass is similar to English cyclic masses dating from the first half of the century by composers such as Frye and Dunstable. Each of the five movements begins with an introductory, two-voice head-motif, to which the full complement of voices replies. Certain sections, such as the *Pleni sunt* and Benedictus and the second Agnus, are duets throughout. These frequent, highly contrapuntal duets, often with asymmetrical phrases, repetitive rhythmic patterns and no pauses, are typical of English music and are a result of the two-voice discant style. In Cornago's Mass the contratenor and tenor share the same range, and both are structural voices. Perfect consonances usually happen between these two voices while the discant moves freely against them in imperfect consonances, except at cadence points where the tenor-discant framework is utilized. The contratenor only occasionally changes its function from structural to discant voice. The latter procedure is somewhat different from that of the English Masses, in which the *cantus firmus* is placed at the bottom of the texture in a tenor-discant framework throughout, with the contratenor complementing the framework with the addition of imperfect consonances.

Determining which characteristics are Spanish in the *Missa "Ayo visto"* presents a serious problem since the next known Spanish Masses (other than the single-movement Gloria by Fernández de Madrid) are at least one full generation later than Cornago's. Spanish composers of the next generation, such as Juan de Anchieta, Francisco de Peñalosa, and Pedro de Escobar, employed few, if any, of the organizational procedures used in Cornago's Mass in their own works. The Franco-Flemish influence that predominated throughout Spain since the tenth century is still evident in the Spanish Masses of the late fifteenth and early sixteenth centuries.

Fernández de Madrid is known to have been a singer at the court of Ferdinand V in 1479 and undoubtedly knew Cornago.[24] From the extant segment of his Mass we can see it is structurally different from Cornago's. The discant and contratenor occupy the same range, (which is considerably higher than in Cornago's Mass), and the tenor is the lowest voice. More significant is the framework of discant-contratenor at internal cadences and discant-tenor only at the final cadence. There are a number of "first-inversion chords," but the structure and the lack of driving, endless phrases with repetitive patterns indicate that the compositional procedures of Madrid's Mass were not directly influenced by the English style.

Perhaps the greatest similarity between the two earliest-known Spanish Masses is the number of chromatic alterations. Although we cannot draw any conclusions about the style of Madrid's Mass from this one fragment, the shifts in this Gloria from the Dorian mode, caused by the addition of E-flat and A-flat, are impressive. Cornago's shifts, on the other hand, are more consistent. The Phrygian mode is frequently superimposed upon a Dorian framework. At cadential points on A, Cornago consistently flats the preceding B of the penultimate chord and then sharps the C in the cadential chord. On the few occasions that these accidentals are omitted in the manuscript, they have been supplied in the edition since the precedents are too numerous to ignore. Only occasionally is G-sharp possible on these penultimate chords. F-sharps and E-flats are used within phrases on a number of occasions. Although English and continental masses often use chromatic alterations, such alterations seem haphazard and do not significantly alter the mode of the piece, as they do in Cornago's Mass.

Cornago's only other sacred work, his motet "Patres nostri peccaverunt," is, like the Mass, historically significant. It is the earliest setting of a text from the Lamentations of Jeremiah by an identified composer (and the only four-voice composition by Cornago). Two other three-voice, anonymous settings, however, are found in the manuscript Montecassino 871 (Montecassino, Archivio della Bodia, cod. 871). Apparently eleven others also appeared in this source, although those folios are now lost.[25] Interest in polyphonic settings of the Lamentations of Jeremiah, then, it would seem, began at the court of Naples in the second half of the fifteenth century, and such settings became increasingly popular in the sixteenth century.

The text for "Patres nostri peccaverunt" is taken from the third lesson from matins on Holy Saturday (*Liber usualis*, p. 759), but it does not use the chant melody. Masakata Kanazawa has suggested convincingly that Cornago's motet, as well as many of the other Lamentations and a number of hymns in Montecassino 871, was not used during the Office but was probably sung during the Passion ceremonies celebrated during Holy Week by Alfonso and Ferdinand.[26]

The harmonic language of the motet reflects the lamenting character of the text and alternates, in a manner similar to that of the songs, between a chordal style at the beginnings of phrases and free polyphony. Structurally, the motet resembles the composer's Mass in its predominant discant-tenor framework with a structural contratenor occupying the same low range as the tenor.

The Secular Music

Cornago's secular music comprises eleven songs, nine of them on Spanish texts and two using Italian texts. They are "¿Donde estas que non te veo?," "Gentil dama non se gana," "Non gusto del male estranio," "Porque mas sin duda creas," "Pues que Dios te fizo tal," "¿Qu'es mi vida preguntays?," "Segun las penas me days," "Yerra con poco saber," "Señora, qual soy venido," "Moro perche non day fede," and "Morte o merce." Cornago's songs provide further witness to his importance as a composer, both by their musical quality and by their wide dissemination in the extant sources. Apart from the anonymous *Versos fechos en loor del Condestable* of 1466, his works are the earliest examples of polyphonic settings of Castilian texts.

Throughout the thirteenth and fourteenth centuries, Provençal, Gallego, and Catalan had been the traditional languages of lyric poetry on the Iberian peninsula, but in the early part of the fifteenth century a new Castilian school developed under Juan II. Alfonso, who was educated at the court of Juan II, customarily spoke Castilian and eventually established this language at his courts of Barcelona and Naples.[27]

The primary form of Spanish poetry from the time of the *Cancionero de Baena*, which was compiled at Juan's court around 1445 by Juan Alfonso de Baena, until the last two decades of the century was the *canción*, a *forme fixe* that originated in the thirteenth-century *cantiga*. The *canción* is typically a lyric poem dealing with courtly love; it should be distinguished from the more rustic texts of the *villancico*, the predominant Spanish form at the end of the century.[28] The *canción* is generally more regular in its meter and verse than the *villancico*. It consists of twelve to fourteen lines divided into three sections: *estribillo*, *mudanza*, and *vuelta*. The *estribillo* is formed by the first four or five lines, usually with the rhyme *abba*, *abab*, or *ababa*. Each verse normally consists of seven to eight syllables but variants of four to nine syllables are also found. The *estribillo* is set to the first section of music (A). The *mudanza* always consists of four lines with the rhyme *cddc* or *cdcd*. The first couplet is set to the second section of music (B), which is then repeated for the second couplet. This is followed by the *vuelta*, which uses the same rhyme scheme as the *estribillo* and is set to the same music. Thus, this form is a variant of a widespread European *forme fixe* (ABBA) found in Italy in the *ballata* and in France in the *virelai* and *bergerette*.

The poets who used this form were primarily from the courts of Juan II and Alfonso I and V. Among them was the most renowned poet of the fifteenth century, the Marqués de Santillana (1398–1458), who served at the court of Aragon from 1412–1418.[29] After Alfonso established his rule in Naples, however, Santillana spent the remainder of his life at Castille. One of Cornago's works, "Señora, qual soy venido," sets a poem by Santillana. Juan de Mena (1411–1456), the author of "Porque mas sin duda creas," was also a member of the court of Juan II and a friend of Santillana. Many of the poets at the court of Juan II were also humanists, and although they are remembered chiefly for their serious poetry and translations of the classics into Castilian, they actually wrote primarily the kind of lyric poetry with elements of wit, sentiment, and unrequited love that was popular at the court. It is therefore not surprising that this lighter poetry made its way to

Naples along with their humanistic works and became the basis for the popular songs there.

Among the poets who worked primarily at Naples was Pedro Torrellas, the author of "Yerra con poco saber," a poem that clearly reveals his dislike of women. According to a legend told in the *Tractado de Grisel y Maravella* of Juan de Flores, Torrellas met his end at the hands of his adversaries, who tore him limb from limb. Another of the poets who served at the Neapolitan court was Suero de Ribera. Isabel Pope has suggested Ribera as the author of "¿Qu'es mi vida preguntays?" (set to music by Cornago) and of "Tanto quanto me desplaze," since in the literary sources (particularly Bibliothèque Nationale, fonds espagnol, MS 226) these poems follow works that are attributed to Suero or are known to be by him.[30]

The extant Spanish literary manuscripts of this era, then, are, for the most part, major anthologies of the poetry produced by the courts of Juan II and Alfonso V of Spain. The manuscripts themselves, however, were not copied until the last quarter of the fifteenth century and the beginning of the sixteenth. As was shown above, only a few of the texts of Cornago's songs can be attributed to known poets at these courts. The other texts are very likely the products of Cornago himself, for musicians during this period were often also poets.

All of Cornago's songs except for "Morte o merce" are in the form of the *canción*. Two of the texts, "Non gusto del male estranio" and "Segun las penas me days," are incomplete, but the intended form of the *canción* is evident from the musical form. Both because their texts are incomplete and because they do not appear in any of the later Spanish manuscripts, it seems likely that these two songs belong to the earliest period of Cornago's composition. The exceptional piece, "Morte o merce," is through-composed. The third and fourth stanzas of the poem appear at the bottom of the page in Escorial B (Escorial, Biblioteca del Monasterio, MS IV.a.24) but not in the other sources. While the first two stanzas fit the music quite easily, the third and fourth present numerous underlay problems; thus, they may not have been intended for the music at all.

The style of Cornago's songs is that of the late Dufay generation. The three voices move at approximately the same rate, and a clear discant style is not completely evident. As in his Mass and in most mid-fifteenth-century chansons, the songs utilize a discant-tenor framework, while the contra remains relatively disjunct, completing the harmonies with either perfect consonances or thirds and sixths as needed. In approximately half of the songs, double leading-tones are used at cadential points, but they are never used consistently throughout a piece. Even in what appear from the sources to be late works, Cornago seems to have turned back to this older style of composition on occasion. Imitation occurs at the beginning of the songs in several instances, but it is rarely continued beyond the first three or four notes. Occasionally in the songs, as in the Mass, Cornago incorporates short canonic sections, as in the final phrase of "Yerra con poco saber."

One peculiar characteristic of many of Cornago's songs is the use of a second ending for the middle section, the *mudanza*. In Montecassino 871 this is indicated by a fermata, but in the somewhat older manuscript Escorial B, repeat signs are used. The character of this second ending ranges from a change in the final, as in "Non gusto del male estranio," to an extended passage in "Yerra con poco saber." This second ending may have been intended for instrumental performance, although there is no direct evidence for this. Isabel Pope, following Liuzzi, has suggested that a final instrumental passage was a trait of Italian *barzellette* and that Cornago may have borrowed this compositional trait from Italian pieces of the same time.[31] Interestingly enough, neither of Cornago's Italian songs, "Moro perche non day fede" nor "Morte o merce," includes this device.

Nino Pirrotta has shown the importance of the "unwritten" tradition in fifteenth-century Italian music.[32] From a culture and time when music played a prominent role, only a surprisingly few polyphonic compositions have survived in manuscripts. Even in these preserved songs, however, evidence of an improvisational style exists. Although the framework of the songs, the discants and tenors, normally contain few or only insignificant variants from one manuscript to the next, the contratenors often vary significantly.

This is especially evident in Cornago's works, since alternate contratenors by Cornago himself or by other composers exist with no fewer than six versions of his songs. In the present edition these six pieces have been grouped together in the Appendix. In the song "Gentil dama non se gana," a second contratenor has been added in the manuscript Madrid, Biblioteca de Palacio, MS 1335 (olim MS 2-I-5), transforming it from a three-voice to a four-voice composition. All three voices of "Morte o merce" have been altered in the manuscript Paris, Bibliothèque Nationale, Rothschild Collection, MS 2973. The discant and tenor have been rhythmically and melodically altered to a certain extent although they still retain their original structure. The contratenor, however, is entirely new and acts more as a bass line than a filler voice.

"Pues que Dios te fizo tal" exists in three versions altogether, each for three voices. The first two versions are equally reliable as compositions by Cornago. Both manuscripts, Seville, Biblioteca Colombina, sign. 7-I-28 and Madrid, Biblioteca de Palacio, MS 1335, contain attributions to him for this piece although the two manuscripts have completely different versions for the contratenor.

The third version of "Pues que Dios te fizo tal" also appears in the Madrid manuscript immediately following the version clearly ascribed to Cornago.[33] The words "Alio modo" are written above the music at the place where the composer's name is usually given by the scribe. This third version, with yet another contratenor to Cornago's piece, exists as a *unicum*. A bit of contemporary confusion has arisen over this version, however, as it exists in modern editions with an attribution to Juan Fernández de Madrid. This confusion originally began with Barbieri's edition of the Biblioteca de Palacio manuscript which contained the words "alio modo" but also gave an unqualified ascription to Madrid.[34] This ascription has passed on to Anglés's subsequent edition,[35] then to Stevenson's authoritative *Spanish Music in the Age of Columbus*,[36] and finally to Pope's article on Madrid in *The New Grove Dictionary*.[37] The only reservation on this accepted ascription is in the commentary on the manuscript by José Figueras which lists the composition as "Anon. [Juan Fernández de] Madrid" in the title index (p. 599) but unfortunately also lists him as the composer of this piece (p. 14).[38]

In the present edition the composition is given an attribution to Cornago (in brackets) since in its source it immediately follows a piece ascribed to him. The style of the newly composed contratenor is, however, not similar to Cornago's other contratenor parts. It is more of a complementing discant than a contratenor and, in fact, is listed as "tiple" (treble). It also uses imitation sporadically and irregularly. Barbieri's ascription to Madrid may have been based on the known use of imitation in Madrid's songs. Madrid's use of that technique, however, is much different from that found in this version of "Pues que Dios te fizo tal." He uses imitation in a very regular way with the imitative voice beginning one measure later in all cases. Also, Madrid does not use a merely complementing discant but favors real contratenor parts. Thus, the identity of the "alio modo" version may still be open to question, but in any case its attribution to Madrid should be discarded.

"¿Qu'es mi vida preguntays?" also exists in a four-voice version in which Cornago's contratenor has been reworked and a bass line added by the composer Johannes Ockeghem. Finally, another example of this "borrowing of a frame" is the song "Señora, qual soy venido." The contratenor of this piece is undoubtedly not by Cornago. The song is ascribed to Cornago and the Spanish composer Juan de Triana (fl. 1478–1483) in the manuscript Seville, Biblioteca Colombina, sign. 7-I-28 and is anonymous in Madrid, Biblioteca de Palacio, MS 1335. A sacred contrafactum, "Infante nos," is written above the text "Señora, qual soy venido," and Higinio Anglés has suggested that this contrafactum text is by Triana and that the composition is by Cornago.[39] It is quite likely that this is indeed Triana's text, since he did write other sacred chanson-motets, but the contratenor may also in fact be by Triana. In this contratenor, the fast-moving rhythms at the beginning of the composition against the imitative discant and tenor are not at all in Cornago's style. In addition, the contratenor in this version descends to a G, a note not used in any other of Cornago's compositions, and though Cornago's pieces occasionally cadence on a unison, this one does so in no fewer than three instances. This is, again, not typical of Cornago's style. These compositions, therefore, may illustrate a tradition of paying tribute to an older master's music by embellishing the least essential part of the composition, the contratenor. They may at the same time give us even stronger evidence of the distinguished reputation Cornago had in his own time.

Sources

Cornago's works are preserved in manuscripts dating from the middle of the fifteenth century to the beginning of the sixteenth and stemming from Bohemia, Spain, Trent, Naples, and other Italian cities.

The complete Mass is copied in Trent, Castello del Buon Consiglio, MS 88, a manuscript written in white mensural notation and dating from the 1460s. The manuscript is an anthology primarily of sacred music by both continental and English composers, but the *Missa "Ayo visto"* is the only work by a Spanish composer contained in it. The folios on which the Mass is copied have been heavily damaged; although the manuscript has been recently restored (thereby considerably stabilizing the deterioration), it does contain a number of large holes. Some of the holes appear to have been produced or enlarged during the restoration process since pre-restoration microfilms and a facsimile clearly show notes that are now missing in the manuscript. In numerous cases the ink has eaten through the paper, so that many of the black notes appear white in photographs, although traces of a black interior can still be discerned. The first two movements of the Mass also appear in the late fifteenth-century Bohemian manuscript Prague, Památnik Národního Písemnictvi (formerly the Strahov monastery) MS D.G. IV.47. There are few variants between these two manuscripts; most of them concern ligatures, accidentals, or repeated notes.

Cornago's songs and his motet survive in nine manuscripts. Although all of these manuscripts are of Italian or Spanish origin, at least two of them are specifically Neapolitan. The more important of the Neapolitan sources is Montecassino 871, an anthology of sacred and secular music. It was not compiled until the 1480s, although its repertory dates from the period of 1430–1480.[40] The repertory, with compositions by English, Franco-Flemish, Italian and Spanish composers, illustrates the cosmopolitan interests at the court. Of the eighteen known composers represented in the manuscript, including such names as Dufay, Ockeghem, Compere, Frye, Dunstable, and Bedingham, Cornago ranks second only to Dufay in the number of pieces transmitted. The manuscript contains seven of Cornago's songs (one of which is Italian) and the motet, as well as Ockeghem's arrangement of Cornago's "¿Qu'es mi vida preguntays?"

There are seven pieces with Castilian text in Montecassino; six of them (including Ockeghem's arrangement) are by Cornago. The other Spanish song, "Viva, viva rey Ferrando," is possibly a contrafactum.[41] Eight other songs with Castilian text are now lost from Montecassino. They appeared in the fourth and fifth fascicles directly after Cornago's "Non gusto del male estranio,"[42] and some of these may also have been the work of Cornago. In the first fascicle, several of Cornago's songs are typically grouped together. This may explain why the archivist of the Montecassino Abbey from 1908 to 1927 added the note "Adsunt in fine cantus sacri et profani auctoribus / Cornago, Dufay, Bernardi, Orelia XVIs," signifying that there were a large number of compositions by Cornago as well as Dufay.[43]

The other Neapolitan manuscript, Escorial, Biblioteca del Monasterio, MS IV.a.24 (Escorial B), dates from the 1460s and is, therefore, the oldest of the manuscripts containing Cornago's music. Most of the repertory consists of French chansons by composers of the Dufay-Binchois generation, although there are also a large number of Italian pieces, including Cornago's "Morte o merce," in it. "Yerra con poco saber" is the only Spanish piece in the manuscript. Only the incipit of the text is given in the contra part, which suggests that the scribe was not familiar with Spanish.

Two manuscripts containing works by Cornago were definitely compiled at the court of Ferdinand V of Aragon, Cornago's last known place of employment. The *Cancionero Musical de la Colombina* (Seville, Biblioteca Colombina, sign. 7-I-28), compiled after 1492, is the second most important source for Cornago's music. Its repertory comes from the period 1470–1495. Cornago's songs in the *Colombina* collection are in the oldest style found in the collection, and are probably his last works. In fact, Seville 7-I-28 shares only one concordance of Cornago's works with Montecassino 871 (other than Ockeghem's arrangement). The *Cancionero Musical de Palacio* (Madrid, Biblioteca de Palacio, MS 1335 (olim 2-I-5) is the latest manuscript to include Cornago's music. With 458 compositions, it is the largest and most important collection of fifteenth-century Spanish music. Its repertory spans the period from 1430 to at least 1503, but it was not copied until the turn of the century. Cornago is certainly one of the oldest composers represented in the manuscript, which contains primarily the works of Encina, Escobar, and Peñalosa. His three *canciones* in the *Palacio Cancionero* are also in the *Colombina* collection, but not in Montecassino 871 or any other Italian manuscript. Therefore, these three songs may be Cornago's last works. They seem to have remained popular in Spain twenty-five years after our last biographical record of him.

The remaining manuscripts are not central sources for Cornago's music. Florence, Biblioteca Nazionale Centrale, Magl. XIX.176 is a manuscript of Florentine origin dating from the 1480s.[44] It contains mostly French chansons and a few Italian songs, and of the ninety-four compositions in it, sixty-three are anonymous. Cornago is represented only by "Moro perche non day fede," his most popular Italian song. The manuscript Paris, Bibliothèque Nationale, nouv. acq. fr., MS 15123 (Pixérécourt) is also Florentine and probably dates from ca. 1500. Pixérécourt gives no attributions, and many of the pieces are *unica*, although it does share a number of concordances, including Cornago's "Moro perche non day fede," with Seville, Biblioteca Colombina, sign. 5-I-43. The majority of pieces in both manuscripts are from the Busnois-Ockeghem generation. Paris, Bibliothèque Nationale, Rothschild Collection, MS 2973, known as the Cordiforme Chansonnier, originated at Savoy between 1460 and 1476. Its repertory consists mostly of French chansons (thirty) and fourteen songs with Italian texts. It too shares a number of concordances with Seville, MS 5-

I-43. The song "Morthe merce" in Cordiforme is a paraphrase of Cornago's version, and the two parts of the song are separated by another composition in the manuscript. Trent, Castello del Buon Consiglio, MS 89 is primarily an anthology of sacred pieces. It originated at Trent in the 1460s to 1480s when Trent was dominated by the Holy Roman Empire. The number of German composers and compositions in this manuscript is relatively large, and it contains many Latin contrafacta of French and Italian chansons. In this manuscript, Cornago's Spanish song "Yerra con poco saber" is given the contrafactum "Ex ore tuo," this time with the text only in the discant. These peripheral manuscripts, then, show Cornago's influence in the growing chapels of the North, where Italian songs were becoming increasingly popular.

Editorial Methods and Performance Practice

The present edition has been prepared in such a manner as to be of use to both the scholar and the performer. Note values have been halved in the sacred music and quartered in the secular music. In the sacred music, and especially in the Mass, the flowing and often melismatic nature of the writing can be rendered better in 3/2 than in 3/4, which would necessitate the use of many eighth- and sixteenth-note values. For the shift from ○ to ¢, the rate of reduction of 1:2 has been retained, since it is not at all certain that ¢ did indicate a tempo twice as fast as that of ○ in Cornago's time. Most likely it represents a ratio of 3:4—three semibreves in perfect time to four in cut time, thus equating the perfect breve to the imperfect longa. If, for example, perfect time were performed at ♩ = 76, then the tempo of the cut time would be ♩ = 132. All final longas have been transcribed as whole-notes in this edition.

Each transcription is based essentially on a single source. Among the sources, those closest to Cornago's time and place of employment are generally the most reliable and have been given the most weight. In cases where two or more equally good sources were available, the existence of a modern edition which used one of those equally valid sources has been taken into account. Whenever possible, alternate versions have been presented here. Musical and textual variants from the principal source are listed in the Critical Notes. The sources have been editorially conflated only when the principal source is lacking textually or musically or when there is an obvious scribal error. Editorial additions in the music and text have been enclosed in brackets. In the edition, ligatures have been indicated by a closed bracket over the ligated notes and coloration has been indicated by an open bracket. Accidentals which are not present in the manuscripts have been placed above the staff, while cautionary accidentals are given in parentheses. All redundant accidentals have been removed in this edition without comment. *Signa congruentiae* which appear in the sources in a variety of scribal configurations have been standardized in the present transcriptions (⌒). They are to be understood throughout simply as cues to the singer that other voices are entering.

The edition of the Mass was prepared from the actual manuscript with occasional recourse to the pre-restoration microfilms and the facsimile. Although the facsimile was poorly made and much of the coloration and most of the dots can no longer be determined, it was helpful on several occasions to confirm or supplement readings. The second source of the Kyrie and Gloria, Prague, D.G.IV.47, helped alleviate many problems in reading Trent 88. The spelling, punctuation, and hyphenation of the Mass texts have been standardized according to the *Liber usualis*, except for the word "Osanna" which instead reflects the source.

The original spelling of the other texts has been retained in the edition, but all punctuation and capitalization have been modernized. In the Texts and Translations within the critical commentary section, only the initial word of each sentence has been capitalized in the Spanish and Italian texts, in accordance with contemporary practices. In the transcriptions, however, each line has been capitalized so that the structure of the poetry can be readily identified by the performer. Each line of the English translation has been capitalized also in accordance with contemporary practices.

The texts in the score have been placed under the phrases to which they correspond in the principal source, and normally only one syllable has been placed at the beginning of a ligature; occasionally this policy has been disregarded when there are no other acceptable alternatives. Many of the songs contain extended melismas after a phrase of text, often at the very end of a section. In a number of cases, an editorial repetition of a text phrase has been provided. The exact manner in which these melismas were performed is not at all clear. The performer who prefers an extended vocalization on the final syllable of the line can quite easily disregard these editorial repetitions. The texts of the songs are placed under the voices with which they appear in the manuscripts. All other voices should be considered instrumental.

The incipit of the motet text was originally placed

in all four voices in the manuscript, but the complete text up to the middle of the word "iniqui[tatis]" was added by a later hand in the altus part. In the edition the text has been added to the top voice, for which it was clearly intended. In both the sacred and secular music, the ensemble calls for various combinations of alto and baritone vocal ranges, although the lowest voices are usually performed by instruments in the secular music and vocalized or played by the organ in the sacred music.

Critical Notes and Texts and Translations

The critical commentary for each piece begins with a list of musical sources with their attributions and indications of texting. The principal source is listed first, followed by concordances, modern editions, and variants for the music. For the motet and the songs, the complete text comes next, together with mention of the poet (if known) and a line-by-line translation. The Spanish and Latin texts were translated by Alejandro E. Planchart and the Italian texts by William F. Prizer. (The texts of the Mass have not been included since they are so widely available.) Following the text and translation, the principal source of the text and concordances are given with a list of modern editions and, finally, the variants.

In the Critical Notes of the music, variants and emendations are given in terms of the original note values. Thus, for example, the variant listed for m. 105 of the tenor in the Kyrie indicates that a minim A in Tr 88 is a semibreve in Strahov, rather than stating, in terms of the transcription, that the quarter-note A of Tr 88 is a half-note in Strahov. This is done to assure the reader of an easy reconstruction of the sources. Measure numbers are listed first in the notes, followed by the number of the note (not the beat) within the measure. Tied notes are counted separately; rests are not counted. Pitches are given in Helmholtz notation wherein middle C=c′, the C above=c″, etc.

The sources cited in the critical commentary are identified as follows:

Musical Manuscripts

CMP	Madrid, Biblioteca de Palacio, MS 1335 (*olim* MS 2-I-5)
Col	Seville, Biblioteca Colombina, sign. 7-I-28
Cord	Paris, Bibliothèque Nationale, Rothschild Collection, MS 2973 (Cordiforme)
Esc B	Escorial, Biblioteca del Monasterio, MS IV.a.24
Facs	Codex Tridentinus 88 (Rome, 1969–70). Facsimile of the manuscript
Fl 176	Florence, Biblioteca Nazionale Centrale, Magl. XIX.176
MC 871	Montecassino, Archivio della Badia, Cod. 871
Pix	Paris, Bibliothèque Nationale, nouv. acq. fr., MS 15123 (Pixérécourt)
Sev	Seville, Biblioteca Colombina, sign. 5-I-43
Str	Prague, Památník Národního Písemnictvi (formerly Strahov Monastery), MS D.G.IV.47
Tr 88	Trent, Castello del Buon Consiglio, MS 88
Tr 89	Trent, Castello del Buon Consiglio, MS 89

Literary Manuscripts and Prints

CG	*Cancionero General de Hernando de Castillo.* Valencia, 1511 and 1520
Espejo	*Espejo de enamorados.* Lisbon, Biblioteca Nacional, Varios reservados num. 177 (Unique copy, ca. 1535–40)
Lo 10431	London, British Museum, MS add. 10431
Lo 33,383	London, British Museum, MS add. 33,383
Ma 3677	Madrid, Biblioteca Nacional, MS 3677 (*olim* M.59)
Ma 2-G-4	Madrid, Biblioteca de Palacio, 2-G-4 (*olim* VII-Y-4)
Ma 2-7-2	Madrid, Real Academia de la Historia, sign. 2-7-2, MS 2. Known as *Cancionero de Bartolomé José Gallardo* or *San Román*
Mod	Modena, Biblioteca Estense, Cod. α.R.8,9 (*olim* XI.B.10)
Pa 226	Paris, Bibliothèque Nationale, fonds espagnol, MS 226

Modern Editions

Amador, *Historia*	Amador de los Rios, Don José. *Historia de la literatura española.* Madrid, 1865.
Amador, *Mendoza*	——— *Inigo López de Mendoza.* Madrid, 1852.
Barbieri	Barbieri, Francisco Asenjo, ed. *Cancionero musical español de los siglos XV y XVI.* Madrid, 1890.

Belcari	Belcari, Feo. *Laude spirituali di Feo Belcari, di Lorenzo di Medici, di Francesco D'Albizzo, di Castellano Castellani e di altri.* Edited by F. Galleti. Florence, 1863.
Bibl. Esp.	*Cancionero general de Hernando del Castillo, 1511.* Edited by Bibliófilos Españoles. Madrid, n.d.
CG	*Cancionero general de Hernando del Castillo.* 1511. Facsimile edition. Edited by A. Rodriguez-Moñino. Madrid, 1958.
DTÖ	Adler, Guido and Köller, Oswald eds. *Sechs trienter Codices.* I. Denkmäler der Tonkunst in Österreich, Band 14–15. Vienna, 1900.
Espejo	*Espejo de Enamorados.* Edited by A. Rodriguez-Moñino. Valencia, 1951.
Gallagher	Gallagher, Patrick. *The Life and Works of Garcia Sanchez de Badajos.* London, 1968.
Gallardo	Gallardo, B. J., ed. *Ensayo de una biblioteca española de libros raros y curiosos.* Facsimile edition. Madrid, 1968.
García de Diego	García de Diego, Vicente. *Marqués de Santillana.* Madrid, 1913.
Haberkamp	Haberkamp, Gertraut. *Die weltliche Vokalmusik in Spanien um 1500.* Tutzing, 1968.
Kottick, *Unica*	Kottick, Edward. *The Unica in the Chansonnier Cordiforme (Rothschild 2973).* Rome, 1967.
MGG	*Die Musik in Geschichte und Gegenwart.* Edited by Friedrich Blume. Kassel and Basel, 1949–1967.
MME	*Monumentos de la musica española.* Barcelona, 1941–.
Morel-Fatio	Morel-Fatio, Alfred P. V. *Catalogue des manuscrits espagnols et portugais dans la Bibliothèque Nationale.* Paris, 1892.
Plamenac	Plamenac, Dragon, ed. *Seville 5-I-43 and Paris N. A. Fr. 4379 (Pt. 1).* Facsimile edition. New York, 1962.
Pope, "Cornago"	Pope, Isabel. "The Secular Compositions of Johannes Cornago: Part I." In *Miscellánea en homenaje a Monsenor Higinio Anglés.* II: 689–706. Barcelona, 1961.
Pope and Kanazawa, Montecassino	Pope, Isabel and Kanazawa, Masakata. *The Musical Manuscript Montecassino 871.* Oxford, 1978.
Pope, "La Musique"	Pope, Isabel. "La Musique espagnole a la cour de Naples dans la second moitié du XVᵉ siècle." In *Musique et poésie au XVIᵉ siècle.* Paris, 1954.
Rennert	Rennert, H. A. "Der Spanische cancionero des British Museums Add. 10431." *Romanische Forschungen,* X(1895–1899): 1–176.
Stevenson	Stevenson, Robert. *Spanish Music in the Age of Columbus.* The Hague, 1960.
Varvaro	Varvaro, Alberto. *Premesse ad un'edizione critica delle poesie minori de Juan de Mena.* Naples, 1964.

The following abbreviations appear in the Critical Notes:

br	breve
err	erroneously
facs	facsimile
lg(s)	longa(s)
lig	ligature(s)
ln(s)	line(s)
m(mm)	measure(s)
min	minim(s)
ms(s)	manuscript(s)
p	pausa
sb	semibreve(s)
sm	semiminim(s)

Missa "Ayo visto"

MAIN SOURCE: Tr 88, fols. 276ᵛ–284ʳ, complete cycle. Frater Johannes de Cornago. "La missa de la mappamundi apud Neapolim et la missa de nostra dona Sancta Maria." Kyrie, fols. 276ᵛ–277ʳ; Gloria, fols. 277ᵛ–279ʳ; Credo, fols. 279ᵛ–281ʳ; Sanctus, fols. 281ᵛ–282ᵛ; Agnus, fols. 283ʳ–284ʳ. CONCORDANCE: Str, fols. 95ᵛ–98ʳ (pp. 191–96), Kyrie and Gloria. Anonymous. Kyrie, fols. 95ᵛ–96ʳ (pp. 191–92); Gloria, fols. 96ᵛ–98ʳ (pp. 193–96).

MENSURATION: Tr 88, Kyrie, discantus, –, ₵, ○; contratenor, –, ₵, ○; tenor, –, ₵, ○. Gloria, discantus, –, ₵; contratenor, –, ₵; tenor, –, ₵. Credo, discantus, –, ₵; contratenor, –, ₵; tenor, –, ₵. Sanctus, discantus, –, ₵, ○; contratenor, –, ₵, ○; tenor, –, ₵, ○. Agnus, discantus, –, ₵; contratenor, –, ₵; tenor, –, ₵. Str., Kyrie, discantus, ○, ₵, ○; contratenor, –, ₵, ○; tenor, –, –, ○. Gloria, discantus, ○, ₵; contratenor, –, –; tenor, –, ₵.

VARIANTS:

KYRIE

Discantus: Mm. 4: rest–6:5, missing in Tr 88 but visible on film. Mm. 59:1–60:1, no. lig in Str. Mm. 61:1–62:1, no lig in Str. M. 88:3, sb e' dotted in Tr 88. *Contratenor:* Mm. 7:1–8:1, no coloration in Str. Mm. 8:2–9:2, missing in Str. M.8:2–3, lig is sb f + sb e + colored br B-flat in Tr 88—scribal error editorially emended. M. 18:1, no coloration in Str. Mm. 25:1–28:1, sb c + sb a lig and br g + dotted br e lig in Str. Mm. 93:3–94:1, sb d colored in Tr 88. M. 94:3–4, superfluous coloration in Tr 88; no coloration in Str. Mm. 105:6–106:1, sb a colored in Tr 88. M. 107:1, min f missing in Str. *Tenor:* M. 28:2, lg in Str. Mm. 76:1–78:1, missing in Tr 88 but visible on film. M. 92:2, missing in Tr 88 but visible on film. Mm. 93:3–94:5, missing in Tr 88 but visible on film. M. 98:1, no dot in Tr 88. M. 98:2, sb p err follows this note in Str. Mm. 99:4–100:1, sb not dotted in Tr 88 or in Str. M. 103:1–2, no lig in Str. M. 105:5, sb in Str. M. 107, min p missing in Str.

GLORIA

Discantus: M. 1:2–3, min stems missing in Tr 88 but visible on film. Mm. 3:2–6:1, missing in Tr 88 although m. 4:1–2 is visible on film—editorially emended following Str. M. 6:p, min c' instead of min p in Str. Mm. 7:6–8:1, sb g' in Str. M. 16:3, b in Str. Mm. 22:2–23:1, missing in Str. M. 26:1–2, coloration in Str. M. 26:4, dot missing in Str. Mm. 40:5–41:2, no lig in Str. M. 48:2, e' in Str. M. 57:2, e' in Str. Mm. 82:1–86:2, missing in Tr 88 and film is indistinct—editorially supplied from Str. M. 89:2, no coloration in Str. M. 89:3, min in Tr 88. Mm. 89:3–90:2, lig on notes 89:3–90:1 in Str. M. 93:1, dotted min in Tr 88. M. 99:1, br e' missing in Str. Mm. 106:2–107:3, missing in Tr 88 but film shows m. 106:2—editorially supplied from Str. M. 111:3, d' in Str. M. 112:2–4, three colored mins are preceded by figure 3 in Str. M. 120:1, no sharp in Tr 88. Mm. 134:1–135:1, two br in Tr 88—editorially emended from Str. M. 137:2, g in Str. M. 138:1, g in Str. Mm. 168:1–169:1, br d' in Str. Mm. 232:3–234:4, br c' + br f' lig, min e', min d' in Str. M. 234:2, missing in Str. M. 258:2, min d' in Str. M. 261:3–5, three colored mins are preceded by figure 3 in Str. Mm. 265:1–266:1, dot missing in Str. M. 267:1, sm in Str and Tr 88. *Contratenor:* M. 1:1, br and sb in Str. M. 3:1–2, perfect br in Str. Mm. 4:3–5:3, missing in Tr 88 but visible on film. M. 6:1–2, perfect br a and sb g in Tr 88—editorially emended according to Str. M. 9:2, dot missing in Str. Mm. 14:6–15:2, missing in Tr 88 and barely visible on film—editorially emended according to Str. M. 42:1–2, no lig in Str. M. 49:1–2, no lig in Str. M. 53:2, punctum perfectionis after br c in Str. Mm. 54:1–57: p, missing in Str. M. 77:1, br c in Str. Mm. 98:1–99:1, lg in Str. Mm. 103:2–104:2, missing in Tr 88 but visible on film. Mm. 110:1 111:1, dot missing in Tr 88. M. 122:1, flat missing in Str. Mm. 140:1–141:1, lg in Str. M. 151:1–2, br in Str. M. 187:1, now missing in Tr 88 and film is illegible—editorially supplied from Str. M. 196:1, now missing in Tr 88 and barely visible on film—editorially supplied from Str. Mm. 211:2–212:1, now missing in Tr 88 and film is illegible—editorially supplied from Str. Mm. 212:3–216:1, now missing in Tr 88 and film barely legible—editorially supplied from Str. M. 229:1–2, now missing in Tr 88 but visible on film. M. 270:1, now missing in Tr 88 and film illegible—editorially supplied from Str. *Tenor:* Mm. 146–148, one lg p and one br p missing in Tr 88 and Str. M. 252:2, dot err after sb a in Tr 88. M. 254:2, f in Tr 88—editorially emended from Str. Mm. 256:1–257:1, lg in Str. M. 270:1–2, br in Str. Mm. 271:1–272:1, lg in Str.

CREDO

The discantus of the Credo omits the phrase "Qui propter nos homines et propter nostram salutem descendit de caelis," but the contratenor, which has an unusually full text for the first half of the Credo, has this text in mm. 56ff. At m. 71 the scribe sought to continue the telescoping of the Credo text, but eventually corrected the text for the discantus, thus we have two sets of words for the discantus from mm. 71–98 as follows:

a. Crucifixus etiam pro nobis sub Pontio Pilato
b. Et in carnatus est de Spiritu Sancto ex Maria Virgine:
a. . . . . passus et sepultus (est).
b. Et homo factus est. Crucifixus etiam pro nobis sub Pontio Pila-
b. to passus, et sepultus est.

Throughout this section the text underlay of the contratenor agrees with that of version b above, that is, the complete text of the Credo, and is the one followed in the edition for both voices.

For the second half of the Credo the contratenor has only the incipit: "Et resurrexit." From the text distribution in the discantus and its relationship with the contratenor it is clear that the phrase "Et in Spiritum Sanctum, Dominum, et vivificantem: qui ex Patre Filioque procedit. Qui cum Patre et Filio simul adoratur et conglorificatur: qui locutus est per Prophetas" was entirely omitted from the Credo. On this see Ruth Hannas, "Concerning Deletions in the Polyphonic Mass Credo," *Journal of the American Musicological Society,* V (1952), 155–186, and W. K. Ford, "Communication," in Vol. VII (1954), 170–172, of the same Journal.

Discantus: M. 43:2, the stem of min e', bottom of br c', and min p can still be seen in Tr 88 despite the hole here. Mm. 45:2–46:1, now missing in Tr 88 and film barely legible—editorially reconstructed from surviving stems only in Tr 88. M. 60:4–5, c' and b in Tr 88 and Str—editorially emended. M. 63:2–4, three black mins in Tr 88—triplet figure editorially supplied by analogy with Gloria, mm. 112 and 261 in Str. M. 160:1–2, err coloration. M. 279:1, err dotted. Mm. 292:1–293:1, hole on first note of lig and appears to read br d', lg e' in Tr 88. *Contratenor:* Mm. 9:4–10:1, sb c' now missing in Tr 88 but visible on film. M. 22:5, b in Tr 88. M. 45:1, min c' emended to b. M. 54:3–4, now missing in Tr 88 but min a is visible on film. M. 199:1, e in Tr 88. Mm. 201:1–202:1, dot missing. Mm. 202: 2–203:2, now missing in Tr 88 and film not clearly legible. Mm. 202:2–203:1, clearly a c.o.p. lig. M. 203:2 was probably sb f, and top of lig is clearly a. Mm. 213:1–214:1, now missing in Tr 88 and film shows an undotted br. M. 226:1, now missing in Tr 88 but barely visible on film. Mm. 227:1–228:1, now missing in Tr 88 but visible on film. M. 234:1, err extra br p after this note. M. 239:2, dot err after the sb. *Tenor:* Mm. 203–210:1, top of lg p and head of lg a now missing in Tr 88 and only barely legible on film. M. 248:1–249:1, no dot. M. 287:1–2, min a, min g, sb g; at end of tenor part, mm. 285:1–288 is recopied as given here.

SANCTUS

Discantus: Mm. 71:2–75:2, a long but narrow gap in Tr 88 has obliterated all of the third space on the staff leaving only the stems and note ends visible but all is visible on the film. M. 217:6–7, sm b, sm c' in Tr 88. *Contratenor:* Mm. 173:1–174:1, partial tear in ms but a dot apparently followed the lig. *Tenor:* Mm. 128:1–129:1, dot missing.

AGNUS DEI

Discantus: Mm. 17:2–18:4, mostly missing in Tr 88 with only stems and a part of mm. 17:3–18:1 and 18:4 visible but film legible up to m. 18:1. Mm. 35:4–36:1, now missing in Tr 88 and film shows scribal erroneous omission. Mm. 39:1–40:1, now missing in Tr 88 but visible on film. Mm. 44:2–45:1, dotted sb d'. M. 93, sb p missing. *Contratenor:* M. 34:2–3, note heads now missing in Tr 88 but 34:2 visible on film. M. 35:4–6, now missing note heads but note heads visible on film. Mm. 69:1–72:1, note heads missing in Tr 88 but 69:2 is visible on film—editorially reconstructed by analogy with discantus part. M. 71:1–2, b, c in Tr 88—editorially emended to correspond with canon. M. 102:2–3, min d, dotted sb f in Tr 88 and Str, making this passage one minim too long—editorially emended to conform with strict canonic imitations throughout Mass. Mm. 146:1–147:1, now missing in Tr 88 except for stem but visible on film.

Patres nostri peccaverunt

UNIQUE SOURCE: MC 871, pp. 248–49. Cornago. MODERN EDITION: Pope and Kanazawa, *Montecassino*, No. 2, p. 108.

NOTES: The scribe provided the piece only with text incipits. The voice designations in the manuscript seem to be somewhat arbitrary, but in any case the main structural voices, in terms of the cadential patterns of the work, are actually the contra-altus and the contrabassus. This may be one of the reasons behind the later addition of a full text to the contra-altus. The discantus has been editorially provided with a full text since it is clearly the most ornamented voice.

MENSURATION: discantus, –; tenor, M. 1: ○; contra-altus, –; contrabassus, –.

VARIANTS: *Discantus:* M. 26:2, a' in MC 871. *Contrabassus:* M. 21:3, c in MC 871.

LAMENTATIONS OF JEREMIAH 5:7 (For use at Third Lesson from Matins on Holy Saturday.)

Patres nostri peccaverunt, et non sunt:
et nos iniquitates eorum portavimus.

(Our fathers have sinned, and are no more:
and we have born their iniquities.)

¿Donde estas que non te veo?

MAIN MUSICAL SOURCE: Col, fols. xvii^v–xix^r. Anonymous. Discantus: text; tenor: incipit; contratenor: incipit. CONCORDANCE: MC 871, pp. 264–65. Cornago. Discantus: text; tenor: incipit; contratenor: incipit. MODERN EDITIONS: Haberkamp, No. 10, p. 137 (after Col); facsimile, plates I–II. *MME*, Querol Gavaldá, XXXIII, No. 10, p. 13 (after Col). Pope and Kanazawa, *Montecassino*, No. 16, p. 150.

MENSURATION: M. 1: ¢, all voices, Col, MC 871.

VARIANTS (all entries refer to MC 871 unless noted otherwise): *Discantus:* M. 6:1–2, min a', min g', min g', min f'. M. 11:1–3, sb a' + dotted sb f' lig, min e', min e', min d'. Mm. 13:4–14:1, two br a. M. 16:4, min c', min b. Mm. 21:2–22:1, lig. M. 22:1–2, min a', min g', min g', min f'. M. 26:3, dotted min f', sm e'. M. 29:1–2, no lig. M. 30:5, min c'. M. 39:1–2, lig. Mm. 39:4–40:2, coloration wrongly applied on br and sb instead of sbr and min. M. 40:3, br. Mm. 42:1–43:1, lig. M. 44:5–6, min e'. M. 47:7–8, sb c'. *Tenor:* M. 7:1–2, lig. Mm. 7:2–8:1, two br f. M. 10:1, two sb f. M. 10:2, flat. M. 13:1, two br f. M. 15:1, two sb d. M. 16:1–3, sb g + sb f lig, br e. M. 17:1–2, no lig. M. 17:2–3, no coloration. Mm. 29:2–30:1, no lig. Mm. 35:3–36:1, no lig. M. 36:1–2, two sb g. Mm. 37:1–39:1, lig. M. 47:2, min f. *Contratenor:* M. 10:3, dotted sb e', min d'. M. 11:2–3, dotted sb c', min b, min b, min a. M. 16:1–2, lig. Mm. 18:1–19:1, lig. M. 24:1, flat. Mm. 31:5–32:1, no lig. M. 32:3–4, dotted min, sm. M. 36:2–3, lig. M. 43:1–2, no lig.

CANCIÓN (Don Diego de Castilla)

¿Donde estas que non te veo?
¿Qu'es de ti esperança mia?
Que a mi que verte deseo
mill años se me fase un dia.

Mas tal es tu fermosura
en tu tierna juventut.
Que con tu gentil fygura
me fieres y das salut.

Comigo mismo querreo
si te desamar podria;
a la fin cativo creo
De quedar [de] tu señoria.

(Where are you that I don't see you?
What's of you, o my hope?
That for me who longs to see you
A day becomes a thousand years.

But such is your beauty
In your tender youth
That with your gracious image
You hurt me and yet give me health.

I myself do not believe
That I could stop loving you
But in the end, I think that captive
I remain by your power.)

MAIN TEXTUAL SOURCE: Col, fols. xvii^v–xix^r. CONCORDANCES: MC 871, pp. 264–265. CG (1511, 1520), 95^v, with a *glosa* by Rodrigo D'Avalos. CG (1511), fol. 121^r, Lo 10431, fol. 2–5, first two verses of the poem are quoted in Badajos's *Infierno d'Amor* in which the *canción* is attributed to Don Diego de Castilla. CG, fol. 183^v, the first verse is quoted by Pinar in *Juego trobado que hizo a la regna dona Isabel con el quel se puede jugar*. *Espejo*, No. 2. MODERN EDITIONS: Bibl. Esp., I, No. 274. CG, fol. 95^v. *Espejo*, p. 63. Gallagher, p. 105. Haberkamp, No. 10, p. 93. *MME*, Querol Gavaldá, XXXIII, No. 10, p. 40. Pope, "La Musique," p. 46. Pope and Kanazawa, *Montecassino*, No. 16, pp. 568–569. Rennert, p. 17.

VARIANTS: Ln 1: no, *CG*, *Espejo*. Ln 2: speranza, MC 871. Ln 3: que mi que, MC 871; a mi que verte desseo, *CG*, *Espejo*. Ln 4: myl, MC 871; me, missing in MC 871; mil, haze, *CG*, *Espejo*. Ln 5: formorsura, MC 871; hermosura, *CG*, *Espejo*. Ln 6: e tu, MC 871; y tu, juventud, *CG*, *Espejo*. Ln 7: figura, *CG*, *Espejo*. Ln 8: hieres, salud, *CG*, *Espejo*. Ln 10: desamar te, *CG*, *Espejo*. Ln 11: quiero, MC 871; mas la fin, *CG*, *Espejo*. Ln 12: quedar de, *CG*, *Espejo*.

Gentil dama non se gana

MAIN MUSICAL SOURCE: Col, fols. vii^v–ix^r. Anonymous. Discantus: text; tenor: incipit; contratenor: incipit. CONCORDANCE: CMP, fols. 27^v–28^r. Cornago. Discantus: text; tenor: incipit; contratenor: incipit; contratenor 2: incipit. MODERN EDITIONS: Barbieri, No. 38, p. 274 (after CMP). Haberkamp, No. 4, p. 126 (after Col). *MGG*, "Cornago" by Higinio Anglés; facsimile of CMP. *MME*, Anglés, V, No. 38, p. 51 (after CMP). *MME*, Querol Gavaldá, XXXIII, No. 4, p. 2 (after Col).

NOTES: The fourth voice in CMP has been added by a later hand and is not authentic. The four-part version appears in the Appendix of the present edition. Variants below are for the three original voices.

MENSURATION: M. 1: ¢, all voices, Col, CMP.

VARIANTS (all entries refer to CMP unless noted otherwise): *Discantus*: M. 2:1, two sb a. M. 24:4–5, dotted min, sm. M. 26:3, dotted sb e'. Mm. 27:3–28:1, br d' + dotted br c' lig. *Tenor*: M. 1:2–3, br. M. 3:1, two sb. Mm. 10:2–11:1, lig. M. 12:1–2, dotted br. *Contratenor*: Mm. 4:3–6:1, lig. Mm. 8:4–9:1, no lig. Mm. 14:3–15:1, dotted sb e. M. 18:1–2, lig. Mm. 19:1–20:1, lig. Mm. 22:2–23:1, dotted br. M. 24:p2, br f + br c lig. Mm. 26:2–27:4, br c + br A + br B lig.

CANCIÓN
Gentil dama, non se gana
otro bien de vos mirar,
syno ver y desear.

El deleyte que se faze,
myrando vuestra beldat.
Se destruye y desfaze,
notando vuestra bondat.

Ansi que mi fin temprano
non lo tiene de causar
syno ver y desear.

Pues que vuestra piedad
para my es tan oscura,
tornad my libertad
con que busque my ventura.

El vos fizo sin enmyenda
de gentyl persona cara
e, sy mata sin contyenda,
tal que otro non vos pintara.

Pues no soys qual presumya
ny yo soy quien ser solya.
Yo vos guardé lealtad,
quando en vos senty verdad.

Mas, agora perdonad
y sabed de parte mya,
. . . .
. . . .

Yo solo sea culpado,
vos queriendo my querer,

y pensad mayor pecado
ser matar que ofender.

Dudando, quyero moryr
fasta lo contrario ver,
no dexando de escrevir
my mote ver y creer.

Plazeme, pues se que sygo
lo que virtud me rrequiere;
desplazeme que fatygo
my querer que no lo quyere.

En el serviçio de vos
toda my vida me fundo,
por lo qual no yero al mundo
ny mucho menos a Dyos.

Vuestros ojos que myraron
con tan discreto myrar,
quietos aun, no dexaron
en my nada por mudar.

Y aun ellos, no contentos
de my persona vençida,
dame tan grandes tormentos
que me atormentan la vida.

Siempre dixe byen de vos,
desde que me conocistes,
tal paresca yo ante Dios
qual sienpre me parecistes.

Quanto a que siento amor
y de como se que duele,
no siento pena mayor
ni que mas me desconsuele.

Tan asperas de sofryr
son mys anguistias y tales
que de mys esquivos males
es el remedio moryr.

Bien se cierto por maneras,
aunque soy mal adivino,
que no diga el buey al vino
no te quyero ni me quyeras.

(Gracious lady, one gains
Nothing else from seeing you
Than the look and the desire.

The delight that one gets
Seeing your beauty,
Is undone and destroyed
Noting your kindness.

Thus my early death
Will be caused by nothing else
But the look and the desire.

Since your pity
Is so obscure to me,
Give me back my freedom
To seek my fortune.

He made you without fault
In your gracious body and face,
And if that gives death without battle,
I would still not change you at all.

Since you are not as I thought
And I am not who I was,
I was loyal to you
While I felt truth in you.

But now, forgive me,
And know from my part,
. . . .
. . . .

I may only be faulted
In wanting you to love my love.
And think, it is a worse sin
To kill than to offend.

I want to die still doubting,
Until I see to the contrary,
Not ceasing to write
My motto: "Seeing is believing."

It pleases me that I know I follow
What virtue requires of me;
It displeases me that I try
My love, which wants no such course.

On your service
I base all my life.
By this I do not offend the world,
And much less offend I God.

Your eyes glanced at me
With such a discreet glance,
But quietly they still left
Nothing unchanged in me.

And even then, not content
With my vanquished self,
They give me such torments
As now disturb my life.

I always spoke well of you
Since you have known me.
Would that I could appear before God
As you always appeared to me.

From what I feel of love,
And as much as I know it hurts,
I feel no greater sorrow,
Nor none that unsettles me more.

So harsh to suffer
Are my sorrows, and they are such,
That from my untouchable ills
The only remedy is death.

I know for certain, by signs,
Even though I am no diviner,
That no ox will tell to the wine:
"I do not like you and please do not like me.")

MAIN TEXTUAL SOURCE: Col, fols. vii^v–ix^r. CONCORDANCE: CMP, fols. 27^v–28^r. First ten lines only. MODERN EDITIONS: Barbieri, No. 38, p. 71. Haberkamp, No. 4, p. 92. *MME*, Anglés, V, No. 38, p. 51. *MME*, Figueras, XIV, No. 38, p. 266. *MME*, Querol Gavaldá, XXXIII, No. 4, pp. 36–38.

Variants (all entries refer to CMP unless otherwise noted): Ln 2: en vos. Ln 3: sino ver i. Ln 4: deleite. Ln 5: Mirando vuestra beldad. Ln 6: y desfaze, missing. Ln 7: bondad. Ln 8: tenprana. Ln 10: sino. Ln 56: desconsuelo, Col.

Moro perche non day fede

MAIN MUSICAL SOURCE: MC 871, p. 275. Cornago. Discantus: text; tenor: incipit; contratenor: incipit. CONCORDANCES: Fl 176, fols. 19^v–21^r. Anonymous. Discantus: incipit; tenor: incipit; contratenor: incipit. Pix, fols 54^v–55^r. Cornago. Discantus: text; tenor: incipit; contratenor: incipit. Sev, fols. 93^v–94^r. Anonymous. Discantus: text; tenor: incipit; contratenor: incipit. MODERN EDITIONS: Haberkamp, No. 97, p. 272 (after MC 871); facsimile of Pix, plate VIII. Plamenac, facsimile of Sev, p. 70. Pope and Kanazawa, *Montecassino*, No. 26, p. 176.

MENSURATION: M. 1: ¢, all voices, Fl 176, Pix, Sev. No mensuration, MC 871.

VARIANTS: *Discantus:* M. 3:1, no sharp in Fl 176, Pix, Sev. M. 4:1–2, no lig in Sev. Mm. 4:4–5:2, br d' in Fl 176, Sev. Mm. 9:3–10:1, no lig in Pix. M. 10:4–5, sb e' in Fl 176, Sev. M. 13:3–4, br in Fl 176. Mm. 15:2–16:1, sb g + sb a lig, sb b in Fl 176, Pix, Sev. M. 18:1–2, no lig in Sev. M. 20:1–2, two mins in Sev. M. 23:3–4, br in Sev. Mm. 29:5–30:1, lig in Fl 176. M. 30:5, min c', sm b, sm c' in Fl 176, Pix; min c', min b in Sev. Mm. 37:3–38:1, lig in Pix. Mm. 46:1–47:1, no lig in Fl 176, Sev. M. 47:1, fermata in Pix. M. 47:3, missing in Pix. Mm. 48:4–49:2, br in Fl 176, Sev; br d', sb c' in Pix. *Tenor:* M. 8:3, no flat in Fl 176. M. 9:2–3, f, c in Sev; f, e in MC 871—editorially supplied on authority of Pix. M. 13:3–4, br in Fl 176, Sev. M. 16:1, dot missing in Pix. M. 19:1, no sharp in Fl 176, Sev. M. 28:3–4, br a in Fl 176, Sev. M. 29:1, dot missing in Pix. Mm. 30:1–31:1, lig in Sev. M. 33:1, missing in MC 871. M. 39:1–2, no lig in Sev. M. 39:1–3, sb f, br g, sb f in Pix. M. 40:4, sb d in Fl 176. M. 45:1–3, sb a + sb f lig, br g in Sev. M. 46:2, flat in Sev. M. 47:3, no sharp in Fl 176, Pix, Sev; br f missing in Pix. *Contratenor:* M. 3:1, no sharp in Fl 176, Pix, Sev. Mm. 3:2–4:1, br in MC 871. M. 5:1–2, br A, dotted sb a, min g in Fl 176; br A, dotted sb a, min f in Pix, Sev. M. 8:2, no flat in Fl 176, Sev. M. 9:2, no flat in Fl 176, Sev. M. 12:1–2, br in Sev. Mm. 21:3–22:1, lig in Pix. M. 22:1–2, no lig in Fl 176, Sev. M. 23:1–3, lig in Pix. M. 27:1, missing in MC 871. M. 27:4–5, two mins in Fl 176. M. 29:2, sb f in MC 871. Mm. 30:1–31:1, lig in Fl 176, Pix. M. 32:3–4, two mins in Fl 176. Mm. 32:5–33:1, no lig in Pix, Sev. M. 33:2–3, coloration in Pix, Sev. M. 36:3, sb g in Fl 176. M. 38:4, br e in Sev. M. 39:3–4, sb d in Fl 176; coloration in Pix. M. 41:3–5, dotted sb f, min e in Sev. M. 41:4–5, min e, min d in Fl 176. M. 43:3–4, lig in Pix. M. 46:2, fermata on lg in Pix. Mm. 47:2–48:1, sb p, sb d in Pix is short by one sb. M. 48:3, no flat in Fl 176, Sev. M. 49:1–2, no lig in Pix.

CANCIÓN

Moro perche non day fede
alla pena che m'acora.
Io te demando mercede;
tu me responde, senyora,
"mal an ay cuy te crede."

Tu sei prisone captiva
de mi triste vida e morte.
Tu sei d'est'alma misquina
che 'n conforte.

(I die because you will not give faith
To the pain that grieves me.
I beg your mercy,
And you, my lady, respond,
"Ill to her that believes you.")

You are both the prison and the chain
Of my bleak life and death.
Of this miserable soul, you are
The solace.)

MAIN TEXTUAL SOURCE: MC 871, p. 275. CONCORDANCES: Fl 176, fols. 19^v–21^r. Pix, fols. 54^v–55^r. Sev, fols. 93^v–94^r. MODERN EDITIONS: Haberkamp, No. 97, p. 104. Pope, "La Musique," pp. 50–51. Pope and Kanazawa, *Montecassino*, No. 26, pp. 577–78.

VARIANTS: Ln 1: da, Sev; dai, Pix. Ln 2: de la pena comachora, Sev; machora, Pix. Ln 3: io ti domanda merce, Sev; i te dumando, Pix. Ln 4: tu mi respondi señora, Sev; respondi segnora, Pix. Ln. 5: ara cui ti, Sev; cui, Pix. Ln 6, persone et catena, Sev; si prison catena, Pix. Ln 7: di mia vita morte, Sev; trista, Pix. Ln 8: missing in Sev; si, mesdrina, Pix. Ln 9: missing in Sev; mi mal et ben et conforte, Pix.

Morte o merce

MAIN MUSICAL SOURCE: Esc B, fols. 91^v–92^r. Anonymous. Discantus: text; tenor: incipit; contratenor: incipit. CONCORDANCES: MC 871, p. 278. Cornago. Discantus: text; tenor: incipit; contratenor: incipit. Cord, fols. 12^v–13^r and 14^v–15^r (each part copied separately). Anonymous. Discantus: text; tenor: incipit; contratenor: incipit. MODERN EDI-

TIONS: Haberkamp, No. 99, p. 277 (after MC 871). Kottick, *Unica*, No. 5, p. 5, and No. 7, p. 7 (after Cord). Pope and Kanazawa, *Montecassino*, No. 28, p. 185.

NOTES: The version in Cord is quite different from the other two and has been therefore included in the Appendix of the present edition. No musical variants are given here for this source.

MENSURATIONS: M. 1:ϕ3, with the 3 cancelled, all voices, Esc B; 3, MC 871; ○, Contratenor, Cord. M. 21: ¢, all voices, Esc B, MC 871; discantus and tenor, Cord.

VARIANTS (all entries refer to MC 871 unless otherwise noted): *Discantus:* M. 18:3, min e'. M. 24:1–2, lig. Mm. 24:4–25:4, br a', min g', min f'. M. 36:1, two sb. M. 37:1–2, lig. *Tenor:* M. 7:1–2, lig. M. 8:1, br, sb. M. 14:1, br g, sb c', M. 19:1–2, lig. M. 24:1–2, lig. M. 24:3–4, lig. M. 29:3–4, lig. Mm. 30:1–31:1, lig. M. 31:1, two br. Mm. 37:3–38:2, lig. *Contratenor:* Mm. 16:1–18:1, now missing, part of folio torn off. M. 19:3–4, sb g err inserted between min g and min f, then cancelled. M. 24:4–5, lig. M. 25:2–3, lig. M. 26:2, two sb. M. 29:1–2, lig. Mm. 31:1–35:1, now missing, part of folio torn off. Mm. 37:5–38:2, br.

THROUGH-COMPOSED

Morte o merce, gentil aquila altiera,
che 'l tempo passa e crudeltà me sfida,
e senza guida solo me trovo in guerra.

Amor, chon l'archo teso, el cor m'a ferra
che romper non se pò l'aspra cadena,
dal primo jorno strecta,
che me conduce a sì crudel martire.

Amor m'asale, credendo a lui fugire,
cerchando escampo, e mi ritruovo in focho.
A pocho a pocho moro e vivo torno.

Sperando, ardendo ormay de jorno in jorno,
lieto vederme solo con dolze riso
da poy che m'a conquiso
mostra mi crudo e non me val defesa.

(Death or mercy, O gentle haughty eagle,
For time passes and cruelty betrays me,
And alone, without guidance, I find myself in battle.
Love, with his taut bow, binds my heart
With his rough, unbreakable chain
Drawn tight from daybreak,
And leads me to so cruel a martyrdom.
Love attacks me, and believing to flee him,
Seeking escape, I find myself again in the flames.
Little by little I die and return to life.
Burning now, day after day, hoping
To see myself with only a sweet smile
But since love has conquered me
He shows me only cruelty, and I have no defense.)

MAIN TEXTUAL SOURCE: Esc B, fols. 91^v–92^r. CONCORDANCES: MC 871, p. 278. Cord, 12^v–13^r and 14^v–15^r. RELATED TEXT: Belcari, Florence (1480); lauda by Feo Belcari, No. XLV, p. 27; "Anima. mia contempla il mio patire: i' sono Dio Jesu dolce signore che per tuo amore in croce vo morire" (Cantasi come—*Morte o merzé, gentil aquila altera*). MODERN EDITIONS: Belcari, No. XLV, p. 27. Haberkamp, No. 99, p. 104; Kottick, *Unica*, No. 5, p. 5, and No. 7, p. 7. Pope and Kanazawa, *Montecassino*, No. 28, p. 579.

VARIANTS: Ln 1: Morte merce, gentil aquill'altera, MC 871; Morthe merce, gentile aquilla altera, Cord. Ln 2: Que 'l, MC 871; he crudelità my, Cord. Ln 3: Che senza guida, Cord. Ln 4: cum l'arco, MC 871; con l'arco teso, del core me afferra, Cord. Ln 5: Que, catena, MC 871; rumpere, chatena, Cord. Ln 6: Del, torno a, Cord. Ln 7, que, sy, martiri, MC 871; a tal murtirio, Cord. Ln 8–14 are unique to Esc B and are written at the bottom of the piece. The syllabification is different from the first set of stanzas, making the text underlay awkward, and has therefore not been set to music.

Non gusto del male estranio

UNIQUE MUSICAL SOURCE: MC 871, p. 343. Cornago. Discantus: text; tenor: incipit; contratenor: incipit. MODERN EDITIONS: Haberkamp, No. 100, p. 279. Pope and Kanazawa, *Montecassino*, No. 84, p. 317.

MENSURATION: M. 1: ¢, discantus.

VARIANTS: *Discantus:* M. 21:2, dot missing. *Tenor:* M. 37:2, br. *Contratenor:* M. 5:2, sb b. M. 37:1, one extra br c'.

CANCIÓN

Non gusto del male estranio
como yo della partida . . .

[Q]ue si la morte nos vi[e]ne
non puede con nos morar.

(I do not like strange evil
As I from departure . . .
That if death comes to us
She will have no place to stay.)

UNIQUE TEXTUAL SOURCE: MC 871, p. 343. MODERN EDITIONS: Haberkamp, No. 100, p. 104. Pope, "La Musique," p. 48. Pope and Kanazawa, *Montecassino*, No. 84, pp. 610–11.

NOTES: The text of this *canción* is incomplete and the form is evident only from the musical structure.

Porque mas sin duda creas

UNIQUE MUSICAL SOURCE: Col. fols. xliv^v–xlvi^r. Cornago. Discantus: text; tenor: incipit; contratenor: incipit. MODERN EDITIONS: Haberkamp, No. 27, p. 174. *MME*, Querol Gavaldá, XXXIII, No. 27, p. 35. Stevenson, p. 224.

MENSURATION: M. 1: ¢, all voices.

VARIANTS: *Discantus:* Mm. 8–32, flat in signature. Mm. 33–48, no flat in signature. *Tenor:* Scribe left out mm. 37:2–42 on fol. xlv^v but recopied entire part on fol xlvi^r. M. 12, no flat in signature after this measure. *Contratenor:* M. 9, no flat in signature after this measure. M. 47:1, an extra br c' precedes the sb d'.

The omission of the flats by the scribe in the tenor and contratenor parts after the first line in the manuscript and the addition of a flat in the discantus after the first line in the manuscript presents a problem. The easiest solution is to omit all the flats from the music, as is done in the edition of the Colombina (*MME*, XXXIII), but since the scribe did include flats in all the voices at one point or another they have been included in this editor's transcription. The flats occasionally cause certain modal problems and ambiguities, although this seems to be a characteristic of Cornago's style.

CANCIÓN (Juan de Mena)

Porque mas sin duda creas
my grand pena dolorida,
dete Dios tan triste vida
que ames y nunca seas
amada ny bien queryda.

Y con esta vida tal
pienso bien que creeras
el tormento desigual
que sin merescer me das.

Pues que muerte me deseas
sin tenerla merescida,
dete Dios tan triste vida
Que amas y siempre seas
Des amada y mal querida.

(So that you will believe without doubt
My great and sorrowful pain,
May God give you such a sad life
That you will love, but will never be
Beloved nor cherished.

And with such a life
I think you will believe
The unequal torment
That you give without my deserving it.

Since you wish my death
When I do not deserve it,
May God give you such a sad life
That you will love but will never be
Beloved nor cherished.)

MAIN TEXTUAL SOURCE: Col, fols. xliv^v–xlvi^r. CONCORDANCE: Lo 33,383, fol. 78^v. Johan de Mena. MODERN EDITIONS: Haberkamp, No. 27, p. 96. *MME*, Querol Gavaldá, XXXIII, No. 27, p. 46. Stevenson, p. 224. Varvaro, No. 49.

VARIANTS (all entries refer to Lo 33,383): Ln 1: dubda. Ln 2: mi. Ln 5: ni. Ln 6: e. Ln 11: merecida. Ln 13: e, nunca. Ln 14: amada ny bien queryda.

Pues que Dios te fizo tal

MAIN MUSICAL SOURCE: Col, fols. xxix^v–xxxi^r. Cornago. Discantus: text; tenor: incipit; contratenor: incipit. CONCORDANCES: CMP, fols. 1^v–3^r. Cornago. Discantus: text; tenor: incipit; contratenor: incipit. CMP "Alio modo," fols. 3^v–5^r. Discantus: incipit; tenor: incipit: contratenor: incipit. MODERN EDITIONS: Barbieri, No. 2, p. 240 (after CMP). Haberkamp, No. 18, p. 20 (after Col). *MME*, Anglés, V, No. 2, p. 2, and No. 5, p. 7 (after CMP). *MME*, Querol Gavaldá, XXXIII, No. 18, p. 20 (after Col).

NOTES: The contratenors in the two CMP versions differ greatly from that in Col and are both given in the Appendix of the present edition. Variants below are for the discantus and tenor only.

MENSURATION: M. 1: ¢, all voices, CMP, CMP "Alio modo", Col.

VARIANTS: *Discantus:* M. 6:3, no flat in CMP, CMP "alio modo." M. 11:4–5, sb f' in CMP, CMP "alio modo." M. 16:4, min d' in CMP, CMP "alio modo". Mm. 16:5–17:1, br d' in CMP, CMP "alio modo." M. 20:1, no flat in CMP. M. 20:3–4, lig in CMP, CMP "alio modo." M. 26:2–3, no lig in CMP, CMP "alio modo." M. 27:1–2, no lig in CMP, CMP "alio modo." M. 31:1, dotted br f' in CMP "alio modo." M. 34:1–2, dotted sb e', min d' in CMP, CMP "alio modo." Mm. 35:1–36:1, lig in CMP, CMP "alio modo." M. 37:1–2, lig in CMP, CMP "alio modo." M. 41, flat signature in CMP. M. 47:3–7, dotted min e', sm f', min e', sb c', min a in CMP, CMP "alio modo." Mm. 48:5–49:1, lg d' in CMP, CMP "alio modo." M. 50:3–4, lig in CMP, CMP "alio modo." M. 51:4–5, sb g' in CMP, CMP "alio modo." Mm. 52:3–53:1, no lig in CMP, CMP "alio modo." Mm. 54:3–55:1, lig in CMP, CMP "alio modo." M. 55:2–5, no coloration in CMP, CMP "alio modo." M. 55:6, sb g' err dotted in Col. M. 56:3–4, min e' in CMP, CMP "alio modo." Mm. 56:5–57:1, lg g' in CMP, CMP "alio modo." M. 59:3, extra br f' inserted in Col. *Tenor:* Mm. 6:3–7:2, lig in CMP, CMP "alio modo." Mm. 12:1–13:1, sb g + sb f + dotted br d lig in CMP, CMP "alio modo." M. 13:2–3, no lig, CMP, CMP "alio modo." M. 14:3–4, lig in CMP, CMP "alio modo." Mm. 17:1–18:1, no lig in CMP, CMP "alio modo." M. 27:1–2, no lig in CMP, CMP "alio modo." M. 27:3–4, br c' in CMP, CMP "alio modo." Mm. 32:1–33:1, dotted br f in CMP, CMP "alio modo." Mm. 35:3–36:1, lg c' in CMP "alio modo." M. 36:2, br d in CMP "alio modo." M. 39:2, sb g in CMP, CMP "alio modo." Mm. 39:3–40:2, lig in CMP, CMP "alio modo." M. 47:1–2, no lig in CMP "alio modo." Mm. 51:1–53:1, sb d' + sb c' lig, br b, br a + dotted br c' lig in CMP, CMP "alio modo." M. 55:3–4, lig in CMP, CMP "alio modo." Mm. 56:1–57:1, lig in CMP, CMP "alio modo." M. 59:1–2, lg d in CMP, CMP "alio modo."

CANCIÓN

Pues que Dios te fizo tal:
graçiosa, dulçe, fermosa,
y mas, honesta,
si te amo desigual,
gentil dama valerosa,
aya rrespuessta.

Respuesta de mi serviçio,
que vivo vida muriendo
trasportado en tu figura,
te demando.
Esperando el benefiçio
que me deves dar, doliendo—
te de mi mal y tristura
en que ando.

Pues que ansi nasçiste tal,
en estremo virtuosa,
di: ¿ que de cuesta
librarme de tanto mal,
tu, señora, tan fermosa,
con tu rrespuesta?

(Since God made you so:
Gracious, sweet, beautiful,
And more yet, honest,
Since I love you unworthily
Gentle, worthy lady,
May I have an answer.

An answer for my service,
For I live life dying
Transfigured by your image,
I ask of you.
Waiting for favors
That you should give me, taking pity
Of my sorrow and sadness
In which I go.

Since you were born that way,
So extremely beautiful,

tell me; what does it cost you
To free me of so much sorrow,
You, o lady, so beautiful,
With your answer?)

MAIN TEXTUAL SOURCE: Col, fols. xxix^v–xxxi^r.
CONCORDANCES: CMP, fols. 1^v–3^r. CMP, fols. 3^v–5^r. *CG* (1511, 1520), fol. 113^v, the first verse is contained in a *villancico* by Alonso de Proaza. *CG*, fol. 155^r, quoted by Pinar in his *Juego de naipes o juego trovado*.
MODERN EDITIONS: Barbieri, No. 2, p. 63. Bibl. Esp., I, 562, II, 90. *CG*, fol. 113^v and 155^r. Haberkamp, No. 18, p. 94. *MME*, Anglés, V, No. 2, p. 2. *MME*, Figueras, XIV, No. 2, p. 248. *MME*, Querol Gavaldá, XXXIII, No. 18, p. 42.

VARIANTS (all entries refer to CMP): Ln 1: fiso. Ln 3: onesta. Ln 6: respuesta. Ln 8: bivo. Ln 13: et tristura. Ln 19: tan graçiosa.

¿Qu'es mi vida preguntays?

UNIQUE MUSICAL SOURCE: MC 871, p. 380. Cornago. Discantus: text; tenor: incipit; contratenor: incipit. MODERN EDITIONS: Haberkamp, No. 14, p. 282. Pope, "Cornago," p. 701. Pope and Kanazawa, *Montecassino*, No. 101, p. 409.

MENSURATION: M. 1: ○, all voices.

VARIANTS: *Discantus:* M. 36:4–5, missing—editorially supplied from the Cornago-Ockeghem version.

CANCIÓN (Suero de Ribera?)

¿Qu'es mi vida, preguntays?
Non vos la quiero negar,
bien amar e lamentar
es la vida que me days.

¿Quien vos pudiera servir
tambien como [yo] he servido?
¿Mi trabaxado vivir
Quien pudiera haver sofrido?

¿Para que me, preguntays?
La pena que he de passar,
pues amar e lamentar
es la vida que me days.

(What is my life, do you ask?
I do not wish to deny it to you,
To love well and to lament
Is the life that you give me.

Who could have served you
As well as I have served you?
My troubled life
Who could have suffered?

Why me, do you ask?
I want to get over this grief,

For to love well and to lament
Is the life that I give you.)

MAIN TEXTUAL SOURCE: MC 871, p. 256–257. CONCORDANCES: MC 871, p. 380 (MC 871–B), Col, fols. xxiv^v–xxvi^r. Pa 226, fol. 35^v. Anonymous, but follows a poem attributed to Suero de Ribera, a poet at the court of Alfonso I of Naples. MODERN EDITIONS: Haberkamp, No. 14 and 102, p. 94. *MME*, Querol Gavaldá, XXXIII, No. 14, p. 41. Morel-Fatio, p. 191. Pope, "Cornago," pp. 701–703. Pope, "La Musique," p. 49. Pope and Kanazawa, *Montecassino*, No. 14, pp. 563–64, and No. 103, pp. 630–31. Stevenson, pp. 220–23.

VARIANTS: Ln 2: la puedo negar, Col. Ln 3: laumentar, Col. Ln 4: das, MC 871–B. Ln 5: pudiesa, Col; podra, MC 871–B. Ln 6: yo, missing in MC 871. Ln 7: trabajado bevir, Col. Ln 8: pudira, MC 871–B; aver, Col; suffrido, MC 871–B. Ln 9–12: missing in Col. Ln 10: que, missing in MC 871–B; suffrido, MC 871–B.

Segun las penas me days

UNIQUE MUSICAL SOURCE: MC 871, pp. 276–77. Cornago. Discantus: text; tenor: incipit; contratenor: incipit. MODERN EDITIONS: Haberkamp, No. 98, p. 274, facsimile, Plate VII. Pope and Kanazawa, *Montecassino*, No. 27, p. 181.

MENSURATION: M. 1: ¢, all voices.

VARIANTS: *Tenor:* M. 5:3, sb g. *Contratenor:* Mm. 20:2–21:1, lg d.

CANCIÓN

Segun las penas me days
contra mi mostrays enemiga
e de la vida que buscais
non syento de que soys tan amiga
[q]ue morir no le fagays.

Yo vos he tanbien servido
quanto non puede ser mas.

(From the sorrows you give me
You show yourself to be my enemy
And from the life that you seek
I do not feel you are such a friend
That you would not kill him.

I have served you so well
To the point that nothing more can be done.)

UNIQUE TEXTUAL SOURCE: MC 871, pp. 276–77. Incomplete text. MODERN EDITIONS: Haberkamp, No. 98, p. 104. Pope, "La Musique," p. 47. Pope and Kanazawa, *Montecassino*, No. 27, p. 578.

VARIANTS: Ln 2: e contra. Ln 3: bivais. Ln 5: fagayo.

Yerra con poco saber

MAIN MUSICAL SOURCE: Esc B, fols. 107^v–109^r. Anonymous. Discantus: no text; tenor: no text; contratenor: incipit. CONCORDANCES: MC 871, pp. 268–69. Cornago. Discantus: no text; tenor: text; contratenor: incipit. Tr 89, fol. 149^r. Anonymous. Discantus: *contrafactum*; tenor: incipit; contratenor: incipit. MODERN EDITIONS: Haberkamp, No. 96, p. 269 (after MC 871). Pope and Kanazawa, *Montecassino*, No. 19, p. 159.

NOTES: The underlay is corrupt in all sources; the discantus should be the texted voice. The *contrafactum* in Tr 89 is a Latin prayer, Ex ore tuo, the text of which is given below the canción which follows here.

MENSURATION: M. 1: ¢ all voices, Esc B; discantus, contratenor, MC 871; discantus, tenor, Tr 89.

VARIANTS: *Discantus:* M. 11:1–2, lig in Tr 89. M. 13:2–3, sb c' in Tr 89. M. 20:3–6, br f', sb e' in Tr 89. M. 20:4–6, min d', sb e' in MC 871. M. 27:1–2, lig in Tr 89. M. 33, br p in Tr 89. M. 34:1–2, missing in MC 871. M. 39:2–3, sb c' in Tr 89. M. 44:1, repeat signs given in Esc B, MC 871. M. 48:1–2, d' and c' mins in Tr 89. *Tenor:* M. 5:2, min e in Esc B. Mm. 7:1–8:1, no lig in MC 871. Mm. 9:3–10:1, lig in Tr 89. M. 10:1, no sharp in Tr 89. M. 11:1–2, no lig in Tr 89. Mm. 15:4–16:1, br d in Tr 89. M. 19:2, no flat in Tr 89. M. 20:1–3, sb a + sb f lig, br g in Tr 89. M. 22:1, br g in MC 871. Mm. 29:1–30:1, br d + br e lig, lg d in Tr 89. M. 31:1–2, lig in MC 871. Mm. 31:3–32:1, lig in MC 871. Mm. 33:1–34:1, missing in Tr 89. M. 36:2–3, no lig in Tr 89. Mm. 37:1–38:1, lig in Tr 89. Mm. 38:2–39:1, lig in MC 871. Mm. 39:2–40:1, lig in MC 871. M. 48:1–2, no lig in Tr 89. M. 49:1, dotted min d, sm e in Tr 89. *Contratenor:* M. 2:1–2, br in Tr 89. M. 3:3–5, missing due to hole in ms in Tr 89. M. 4:1–2, no lig in Tr 89. Mm. 5:3–6:2, lig in Tr 89. M. 6:2–5, br c', sb b in Tr 89. M. 8: 1–2, no lig in Tr 89. Mm. 32:3–33:1, sb c + sb e lig, br d in Tr 89. M. 41:2, d err br in Esc B; br p in MC 871. M. 43:1–2, lig in Tr 89. M. 49:3, min d, min c in Tr 89.

CANCIÓN (Pedro Torrellas)

Yerra con poco saber
quien toviere tal creencia,
que firmeza de muger
a los peligros d'ausencia,
se pueda mucho tener.

Con fe de presta tornada,
non cessando el escrevir,
bien podra alguna guardada
dos o tres dias bevir.

Mas a la mas detener
no les abasta la ciencia,

por qu'es su natural ser
tienen aquesta dolencia,
qu'es, olvidanca sin ver.

(He errs from little knowledge
Who holds to such belief,
That the steadfastness of a woman
In the perils of an absence
Can be held to be of much worth.

With faith of a prompt return,
And never ceasing to write,
Perhaps a well kept one
Will survive two or three days.

But for the rest, it is not enough
To give them freedom,
For it is their natural being
That they have this defect,
That is, to forget what they don't see.)

MAIN TEXTUAL SOURCE: MC 871, pp. 268–69. CONCORDANCES: Esc B, fol. 107^v–109^r; incipit in contratenor only, Yera con pocho. Mod, fol. 27^v, Juan de Mena *poeta excellentissimo.* Lo 10431, fol. 108^r, *canción*-Torrellas. CG, fol. 178^v, *canción de Torrellas.* MODERN EDITIONS: Bibl. Esp., II, No. 856, p. 70. *CG*, fol. 178^v. Haberkamp, No. 96, p. 104. Pope, "La Musique," p. 48. Pope and Kanazawa, *Montecassino*, No. 19, pp. 572–73. Rennert, No. 298, p. 124. Varvaro, No. 72.

VARIANTS: Ln 6: cierta tornada, Lo 10431. Ln 7: scrivir, MC 871; de escrevir, Mod; ell, CG, Lo 10431. Ln 8–14: missing in MC 871. Ln 8: puede alcuna muy guardada, Mod. Ln 9: meses bevir, Lo 10431; cinco o seis meses bivir, Mod. Ln 10: pero alas mas, Mod. Ln 11: basta, Lo 10431; basta ninguna ciencia, Mod. Ln 12: porque su, Mod, Lo 10431; y ser, Lo 10431. Ln 13: tiene, Mod. Ln 14: que es, Mod.

LATIN PRAYER, *contrafactum*

Ex ore tuo, sanctissima virgo, procedet consolatio miserorum, redemptio captivorum, liberatio dampnatorum, salus vinculorum filiorum adae. Copiossam caritate virgo salutari se fecit.

(From your mouth, o most holy Virgin, comes the consolation of the afflicted, the redemption of the captive, the freedom of the condemned, the salvation of the bound sons of Adam. The Virgin of Salvation makes herself copious in charity.)

UNIQUE TEXTUAL SOURCE: Tr 89, fol. 149^r. *Contrafactum* to *Yerra con poco saber.*

APPENDIX: Alternate Versions and Double Attributions

Gentil dama non se gana (after CMP)

SOURCE: CMP, fols. 27^v–28^r. Cornago.

NOTES: The contra I is spurious, added by a later hand. See p. xx for full notes on texting, editions, variants, and text translation.

Morthe merce (after Cordiforme)

SOURCE: Cord, fols. 12^v–13^r and 14^v–15^r. Anonymous.

NOTES: All three voices differ considerably from those in the other sources. This manuscript is less reliable than Esc B or MC 871. See p. xxii for full notes on texting, editions, and text and translation.

Pues que Dios te fiso tal (after CMP)

SOURCE: CMP, fols. 1^v–3^r. Cornago.

NOTES: This source is no less reliable than Col, but the contra parts differ considerably between them. See p. xxiv for full notes on texting, editions, variants in the discantus and tenor, and text and translation.

Pues que Dios te fizo tal ([Cornago])

SOURCE: CMP, fols. 3^v–5^r. "Alio modo"

NOTES: This source immediately follows the Cornago version (listed above) in the manuscript. The discantus and tenor parts are identical, but the tiple differs considerably from its counter-part, the contratenor, in the other two versions. See p. xxiv for full notes on texting, editions, variants in the discantus and tenor parts, and text and translation.

¿Qu'es mi vida preguntays? (Cornago-Ockeghem)

MAIN SOURCE: MC 871, pp. 256–57. Cornago-Oquegan. Discantus: text; tenor, contra-altus, contrabassus: incipits. CONCORDANCE: Col, fols. xxiv^v–xxvi^r. Anonymous. Discantus: text; tenor, contra-altus, contrabassus: incipits. MODERN EDITIONS: Haberkamp, No. 102, p. 145 (after Col). *MME*, Querol Gavaldá, XXXIII, No. 14, p. 13 (after Col). Pope, "Cornago," p. 703 (after MC 871). Pope and Kanazawa, *Montecassino*, No. 10, p. 131; facsimile, Plate II. Stevenson, p. 220 (After Col).

MENSURATION: M. 1: ○, all voices, Col; no mensuration, MC 871.

VARIANTS (all entries refer to Col unless noted otherwise): *Discantus:* Mm. 12:2–25:1, written a third too high in MC 871. M. 21:3–4, min e', min d'. M. 24:7, sm c', sm b. *Tenor:* M. 13:5, min a. Mm. 14:1–15:1, no lig. M. 17:2, no flat. M. 35:1–2, br d'. *Contra-altus:* M. 6:1, two sb. M. 11:3, min B err in Col, MC 871. M. 13:3, sm c err in Col, MC 871. M. 13:4, min d. M. 33:2, min e. M. 34:2, min g. Mm. 35:4–36:1, sb a, min p in MC 871. M. 38:3, min a. Mm. 42:2–43:1, no lig. *Contrabassus:* M. 7:3–4, dotted min B, sm c. M. 19:1, no flat. M. 32:1, no flat. Mm. 34:1–35:1, lig. M. 35:2, no flat.

Text and translation, see p. xxv.

Señora, qual soy venido (Cornago-Triana)

MAIN MUSICAL SOURCE: Col, fols. xxxvi^v–xxxviii^r. Cornago-Triana. Discantus: texts *Señora, qual soy venido-Infante nos*; tenor: incipit; contratenor: incipit. CONCORDANCE: CMP, fols. 38^v–39^r. Anonymous. Discantus: text; tenor: incipit; contratenor: incipit. MODERN EDITIONS: Barbieri, No. 42, p. 292 (after CMP). Haberkamp, No. 22, p. 163 (after Col). *MME*, Anglés, V, No. 52, p. 72 (after CMP). *MME*, Querol Gavaldá, XXXIII, No. 22, p. 27 (after Col).

MENSURATION: M. 1: ¢, all voices, CMP; discantus only, Col.

VARIANTS (all entries refer to CMP unless otherwise noted): *Discantus:* M. 3:1, no flat. M. 4:4, no sharp in Col. M. 6:1–2, br a'. M. 8:2, sm d', sm c'. Mm. 8:4–9:1, no lig. Mm. 10:3–11:1, lg d'. Mm. 12:1–. 13:1, no lig. M. 13:2–3, lig. Mm. 15:4–16:1, dotted sb, sb. Mm. 16:3–17:1, lg g'. M. 21:1–2, br. M. 21:3–4, no lig. M. 22:1–2, no lig. M. 22:3–4, lig. Mm. 28–37, no flat signatures in Col. M. 28:1–2, no lig. Mm. 32:2–33:1, dotted br. M. 34:3–4, lig. M. 36:2, min c', min b-flat in Col. M. 37:1–2, lg. M. 42:3–4, lig. M. 43:2–4, dotted sb b', sm a', sm g'. *Tenor:* M. 4:1–2, br. M. 5:1–2, lig. Mm. 5:3–6:1, lig. M. 8:1–2, lig. Mm. 10:2–11:1, lg. Mm. 11:2–12:1, lig. M. 12:2–3, lig. M. 13:2–3, br g. Mm. 16:2–17:1, lg. M. 19:1, no flat in Col, two sb b in CMP. M. 23:1–2, lig. M. 23:3–4, lig. Mm. 24:3–25:1, lig. Mm. 28–44, flat signature in Col and CMP. M. 33:3–4, lig. M. 34:1–2, no lig. M. 37:1–2, lg. M. 40:1, two sb. M. 42:1–2, no lig. *Contratenor:* Two flats in the signature on the first staff of Col (i.e., mm. 1–5), one flat in the signature on the second staff of Col (i.e., mm. 6–13:1), no flats in Col. thereafter (i.e., after m. 13); one flat signature throughout in CMP. Mm. 3:4–4:1, lig. M. 9:3–4, no lig. Mm. 13:1–14:1, br d + br e + br d lig. Mm. 16:3–17:1, lg G. M. 17:2–3, br d. Mm. 19:2–20:1, lig. M. 35:2, c. M. 38:1–3, sb, min, min. M. 41:3–4, lig.

CANCIÓN (Marqués de Santillana)

Señora, qual soy venido
tal me parto,
de trabajos, mas que farto,
dolorido.

¿Quien non se farta de males
y de vida desplasiente?
A las penas desiguales
sufro, callado y paciente.

Siño yo, que sin sentido,
me diran
los que mis daños sabran,
e perdido.

(Lady, as I came
So I go,
More than fed up with labors,
Pained.

Who does not get fed up with sorrows
And with an unpleasant life?
The unequal sorrows
I suffer quietly and patiently.

Except me, that senseless
I will be called
By those who know my sorrows,
And lost.)

MAIN TEXTUAL SOURCE: Col, fols. xxxvi^v–xxxvii^r. CONCORDANCES: CMP, fol. 38^v–39^r. Ma 2-G-4, fol. 242^r. Ma 3677, fol. 213^r. Ma 2-7-2, fol. 152^r. MODERN EDITIONS: Amador, *Historia*, VI, p. 538. Amador, *Mendoza*, p. clxi (incipit No. 34) and p. clxiii (incipit No. 41). García de Diego, p. 227. Haberkamp, No. 22, p. 95. *MME*, Figueras, XIV:2, No. 52, p. 273. *MME*, Querol Gavaldá, XXXIII, No. 22, p. 44.

VARIANTS: Ln 1: senyora, Ma 2-7-2. Ln 3: de cuydados, Ma 2-G-4, Ma 3677. Ln 4: e dolorido, Ma 2-G-4, Ma 3677. Ln 6: y vida desplaziente, CMP; e de vida, Ma 2-G-4, Ma 3677. Ln 7: de las penas desiguales, CMP; e las penas desyguales, Ma 2-G-4, Ma 3677. Ln 8: sufre, callando paciente, CMP, Ma 2-G-4, Ma 3677. Ln 9: sinon, Ma 3677. Ln 11: males veran, CMP; males sabran, Ma 2-G-4, Ma 3677. Ln 12: ay perdido, CMP. Ma 2-G-4 and Ma 3677 contain two extra stanzas.

CANCIÓN (Triana?) *Contrafactum*

Infante nos es nascido
con toda sabiduria,
a nosotros ofrecido
para darnos alegria.

Con amor y caridad,
este nino tan gracioso
vino ledo y gozoso
con perfecta umilidad.

A tomar umilidad,
y nascio en este dia
sin perder virginydad
su madre, Santa Maria.

(A child is born to us
With all wisdom,
Offered to us
To give us joy.

With love and charity
This child so gentle
Came joyful and happy
With perfect humility.

To take human shape,
And was born this day,
Without his mother, Holy Mary,
Losing her virginity.)

UNIQUE TEXTUAL SOURCE: Col, fols. xxxvi^v–xxxvii^r. *Contrafactum* to "Señora, qual soy venido."

Acknowledgments

Thanks are due to the librarians at the Castello del Buon Consiglio in Trent, Italy, for their generous assistance. I owe special gratitude to my advisor, Alejandro Planchart, without whose help this project would not have been possible, and also to William Prizer and to Margaret Bent for their continual guidance and support. Finally, I gratefully wish to thank my husband and family, whose patience and encouragement were unending.

Rebecca L. Gerber

Notes

1. A notice of this activity appears in the archives of Naples on November 30, 1455, as reported in Camillo Minieri-Riccio, "Alcuni fatti al Alfonso I di Aragona dal 15 di aprile di 1437 al 31 di maggio di 1458," *Archivio storico per le province napoletana* VI (1881): 441.

2. Isabel Pope, "La musique espagnole à la cour de Naples dans la seconde moitié du XVe siècle," *Musique et poésie au XVIe siècle* (Paris, 1954), pp. 39–40.

3. Higinio Anglés, *La música en la corte de los Reyes Católicos*, Monumentos de la música española, I, (Madrid, 1941): 17–19.

4. Minieri-Riccio, "Alcuni fatti," p. 437. The report has been confirmed by Allan Atlas in "Alexander Agricola and Ferrante I of Naples," *Journal of the American Musicological Society* XXX (1977): 318. Below is the citation of the original Italian from Minieri-Riccio:

> Alfonso spedisce a Roma per missione affidatagli Don Giovanni Dixer Signore della baronia di Ixer in Aragona, che ora trovasi nella sua Corte, dove ancora sta Lazzaro de Andronico greco di Constantinopoli, maestro Luigi Cardona, maestro in teologia con l'annua pensione di ducati 300; e Fra Giovanni Cornago dell'ordine di S. Francesco con la pensione di ducati 300 annue. (Cedole 29, fol. 323, 406 e Cedole 28, fol. 232, 237)

5. The Pope in question was Calixtus III (1455–1458), the Spanish cardinal Alfonso Borgia, and uncle of Alexander VI. See Alan Ryder, *The Kingdom of Naples under Alfonso the Magnanimous: The Making of a Modern State* (Oxford, 1976), p. 38.

6. The record is found in the few remaining fragments of the Aragonese *Cedole di tesoreria* in the Archivio di Stato, Naples. I would like to thank Allan Atlas for sending me this citation.

7. See Nicola Barone, "Le cedole di tesoreria dell'Archivio di Stato di Napoli dall'anno 1460 al 1504," *Archivio storico per le province napoletana* IX (1884): 209. The document, taken from Registro 44, fols. 201–202, reads as follows:

> Ed al Reverendo frate Giovanni Cornago elemosiniere maggiore del Re, si danno 10d. ed un tarì per pagare la confezione degli abiti di drappo tolti dalla guardaroba della corte per 34 poveri, che il Re vuole si vestano nel Castelnuovo di Napoli; e 25d. per l'offerta, che il Re farà nel venerdì santo, adorando la vera croce in Castelnuovo.

8. For information concerning Dufay's duties as cleric and composer, see Craig Wright, "Dufay at Cambrai: Discoveries and Revisions," *Journal of the American Musicological Society* XXVIII (1975): 186.

9. Anglés, *La música*, p. 24.

10. Transcribed in Robert Stevenson, *Spanish Music in the Age of Columbus* (The Hague, 1960), p. 205, from the manuscript Madrid, Biblioteca Nacional, MS 2092, fols. 234v–235r.

11. Ann Livermore, *A Short History of Spanish Music* (New York, 1972), p. 51.

12. Transcribed in Stevenson, *Spanish Music*, pp. 178–179.

13. To date, only the first Kyrie of Cornago's Mass has been transcribed, again by Robert Stevenson, *Spanish Music*, p. 123.

14. Concerning the dating of this Mass, see Alejandro E. Planchart, "Guillaume Dufay's Masses: A View of the Manuscript Traditions," *Papers Read at the Dufay Quincentenary Conference, Brooklyn College, December 6–7, 1974* (Brooklyn, New York, 1976), p. 38.

15. Described by Reinhard Strohm, "Ein unbekanntes Chorbuch des 15. Jahrhunderts," *Die Musikforschung* XXI (1968): 41.

16. The Italian word *mappamundo* translates as globe or map of the world, although, at least in this century, it normally refers to a globe. Circular maps are known to have existed by at least 1450 in Italy even though it was not generally believed that the world was round before Columbus's, and later Magellan's, expeditions. See Edward L. Stevenson, *A Description of Early Maps, Originals and Facsimiles (1452–1611) Being a Part of the Permanent Wall Exhibition of the American Geographical Society* (New York, 1921) and Marcel Destombes, "Fragments of Two Medieval World Maps at the Topkapu Saray Library," *Imago Mundi* XII (1955): 150.

17. Alessandro D'Ancona, ed., *La poesia popolare italiana* (Livorno, 1906: Reprint ed., Bologna, 1967), pp. 475–476.

18. This was first pointed out by Federico Ghisi in "Stram-

botti e laude nel travestimento spirituale della poesia musicale del Quattrocento," *Collectanea historiae musicae* I: (Florence, 1953), 61–62. Ghisi also attempted to reconstruct part of the song from the third statement of the *cantus firmus* of the Gloria of the Mass.

19. Feo Belcari, *Laude spirituali di Feo Belcari, di Lorenzo di Medici, di Francesco D'Albizzo, di Castellano Castellani e di altri* (Florence, 1863), No. CLXV, p. 75. For the dating of this print see Joseph J. Gallucci, Jr., "Festival Music in Florence *ca. 1480—ca. 1520: Canti carnascialeschi, trionfi*, and Related Forms" (Ph.D. diss., Harvard University, 1966), I: 41.

20. There are minor variants between the two versions. In Example 1, taken from the Gloria, m. 12 is a breve d' in the Credo, and m. 14:4 reads b' in all three Credo *cantus firmus* statements as well as in the Osanna 1 but is an a' in the other versions.

21. William F. Prizer, "Performance Practices in the Frottola," *Early Music* III (1975): 228. The final note d' has been added as a second ending, similar to the change of endings in the Petrucci *frottole* prints.

22. Concerning earlier attempts at dating the Mass from known dates of contemporary maps, see André Pirro, *Histoire de la musique de la fin du XIVe siècle à la fin du XVIe* (Paris, 1940), p. 157; Gustav Reese, *Music in the Renaissance*, rev. ed. (New York, 1959), p. 576; and Robert Snow, "The Manuscript Prague, Strahov Monastery, D.G.IV.47." (Ph.D. diss., University of Illinois, 1968), pp. 105–107.

23. In her article on Cornago in *The New Grove Dictionary*, Isabel Pope infers that the two parts of the superscription refer to two separate Masses by Cornago; the first part, "La missa de la mappa mundi apud Neapolim," referring to the *Missa "Ayo visto*," and the second part, "et la missa de nostra dona Sancta Maria," to a Mass-motet cycle based on the *cantus firmus "Meditatio cordis"* (which is never listed by name in her article). The motet of the cycle, "Gaude Maria," immediately follows the *Missa "Ayo visto"* in Trent 88 (*Denkmäler der Tonkunst in Österreich*, vols. 14–15 (Vienna, 1900), no. 416–417) with which Robert Snow has identified a corresponding Mass cycle in Strahov (fols. 85v–92r), as nos. 87–90 in "The Manuscript Prague," transcribed on pp. 277–311. See also his article "The Mass-Motet Cycle: A Mid-Fifteenth-Century Experiment," *Essays in Musicology in Honor of Dragan Plamenac on His 70th Birthday* (Pittsburgh, 1969), pp. 301–320. The Mass-motet cycle was, in fact, written for Masses for the Virgin. According to Snow, its *cantus firmus* "is a responsory formerly used at matins for the feast of the Assumption and that of the tract of the Marian votive Mass for Lent" ("The Manuscript Prague," p. 91). The reference to the Virgin in the superscription, copied only above Cornago's Mass, is undoubtedly the sole responsibility of the Trent scribe. The Marian motet may have been copied with Cornago's Mass in order to group Marian compositions together for use at Marian services. Any attempt to group composers' works together in Trent 88 is non-existent but the grouping of works for a certain feast is common, e.g., the Proper cycles. The *Missa "Meditatio cordis"* is probably the work of an English composer, also suggested by Snow ("The Manuscript Prague," pp. 92–93) and with which I fully agree. Marian motets during this period are frequently English. Also, the Mass is lacking a Kyrie and has bipartite structures and notational peculiarities typical of English composers. Any similarities in style between the *Missa "Ayo visto"* and the *Missa "Meditatio cordis"* are merely an incidental result of Cornago's familiarity with English music.

24. Stevenson, *Spanish Music*, p. 179.

25. Isabel Pope and Masakata Kanazawa, *The Musical Manuscript Montecassino 871* (New York, 1978), pp. 21–28.

26. Ibid., p. 45.

27. Ibid., p. 90.

28. For more background on the history and development of the *canción* and *villancico*, see Isabel Pope, "Musical and Metrical Form of the *villancico*," *Annales musicologiques* II (1954): 189–214, and Pierre Le Gentil, *La poésie lyrique espagnole et portugaise à la fin du moyen-âge: Les formes* (Rennes, 1952), pp. 244–290.

29. David Foster, *The Marqúes de Santillana* (New York, 1971), p. 13.

30. Pope and Kanazawa, *The Musical Manuscript*, p. 564.

31. Ibid., p. 96.

32. On the oral tradition in Italy, see William F. Prizer, *Courtly Pastimes: The Frottole of Marchetto Cara* (Ann Arbor, 1980), pp. 63–64; Nino Pirrotta, "Tradizione orale e scritta nella musica," *L'Ars Nova italiana del Trecento* III: (1970), 431–432; and idem, "Music and Cultural Tendencies in 15th-Century Italy," *Journal of the American Musicological Society* XIX (1966): 127–166.

33. Cornago's piece appears as No. 2 in Anglés's edition of the manuscript Madrid, Biblioteca de Palacio, MS 1335 in Monumentos de la música española V, and the "alio modo" version appears as No. 5. The two pieces listed as Nos. 3 and 4 were added by a later hand at the bottom of the folios on which Cornago's song and the "alio modo" piece appear. Therefore, Cornago's song and the "alio modo" version were originally consecutive compositions.

34. *Cancionero musical español de los siglos XV y XVI* (Madrid, 1890), pp. 63 and 243.

35. *La música en la corte de los Reyes Católicos: Cancionero musical de Palacio*, Monumentos de la música española, V and X (Madrid, 1947–1951), p. 7.

36. Stevenson, *Spanish Music*, p. 240–242.

37. *The New Grove Dictionary*, s.v. "Madrid."

38. *La música en la corte de los Reyes Católicos: Cancionero musical de Palacio*, Monumentos de la música española, vol. XIV (Barcelona, 1965).

39. Anglés, *La música*, p. 104.

40. Pope and Kanazawa, *The Musical Manuscript*, p. 1.

41. Ibid., pp. 639–640.

42. Ibid., pp. 21–27.

43. Ibid., p. 3.

44. During the 1450s, there were close though not always friendly ties between Florence and Naples. In June 1451, when war seemed imminent between the two states, the Florentines requested a visit by the singers of the king of Naples to improve relations. See Frank D'Accone, "The Singers of San Giovanni in Florence During the 15th Century," *Journal of the American Musicological Society* XIV (1961): 318, documents nos. 11–15.

COMPLETE WORKS

Missa "Ayo visto"

Gloria

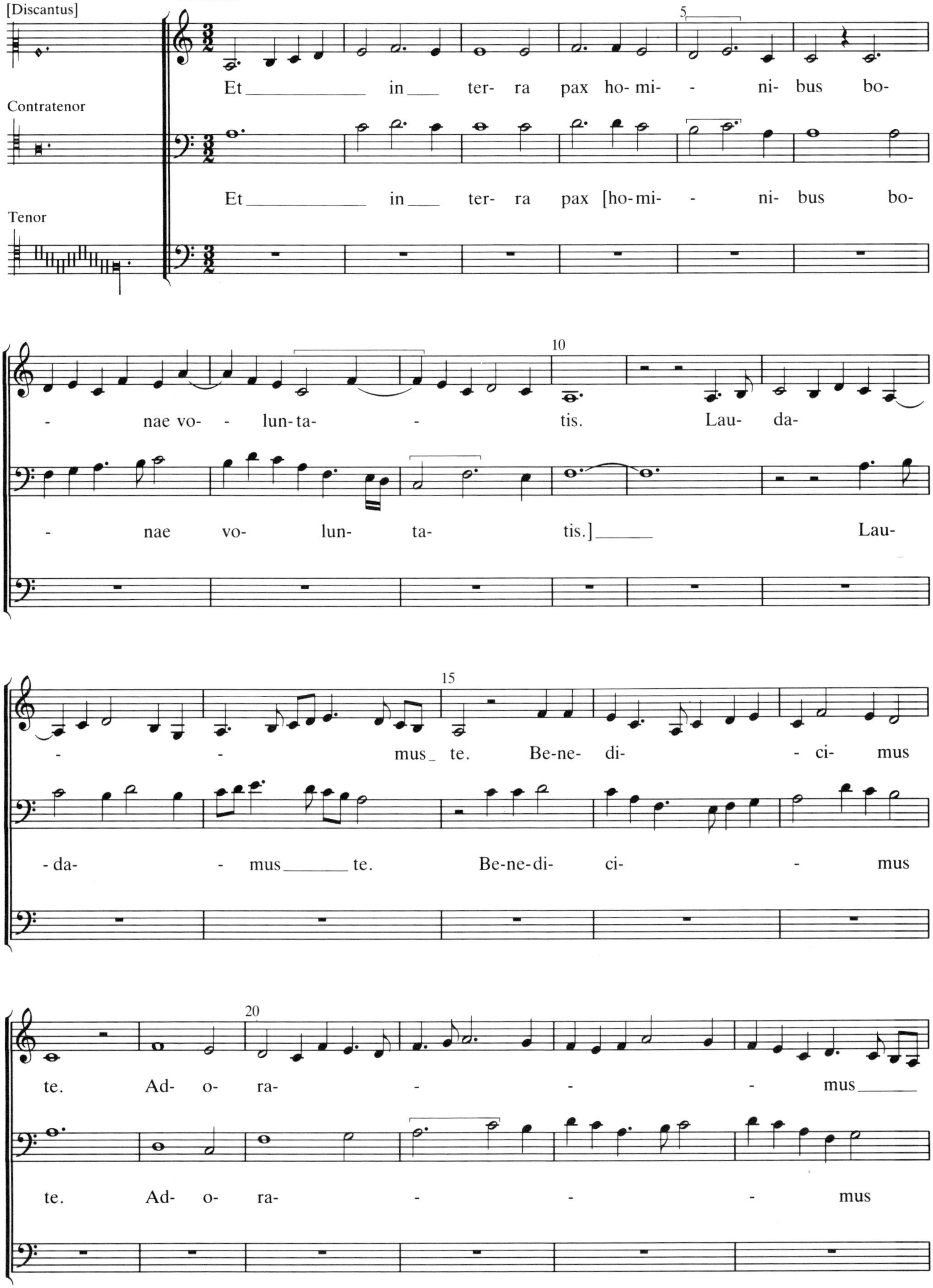
[Discantus]
Contratenor
Tenor
Et in ter- ra pax ho-mi- - ni- bus bo-
Et in ter- ra pax [ho-mi- - ni- bus bo-
- nae vo- - lun-ta- - tis. Lau- da-
- nae vo- lun- ta- tis.] Lau-
- - mus te. Be-ne- di- - ci- mus
- da- - mus te. Be-ne-di- ci- - mus
te. Ad- o- ra- - - - mus
te. Ad- o- ra- - - - mus

Et in terra. Ayo visto lo mappa mundi

Ayo visto lo mappa mundi et la carta di navigare mà chichilia me pare

Credo

Patrem. Ayo visto.

Et resurrexit.

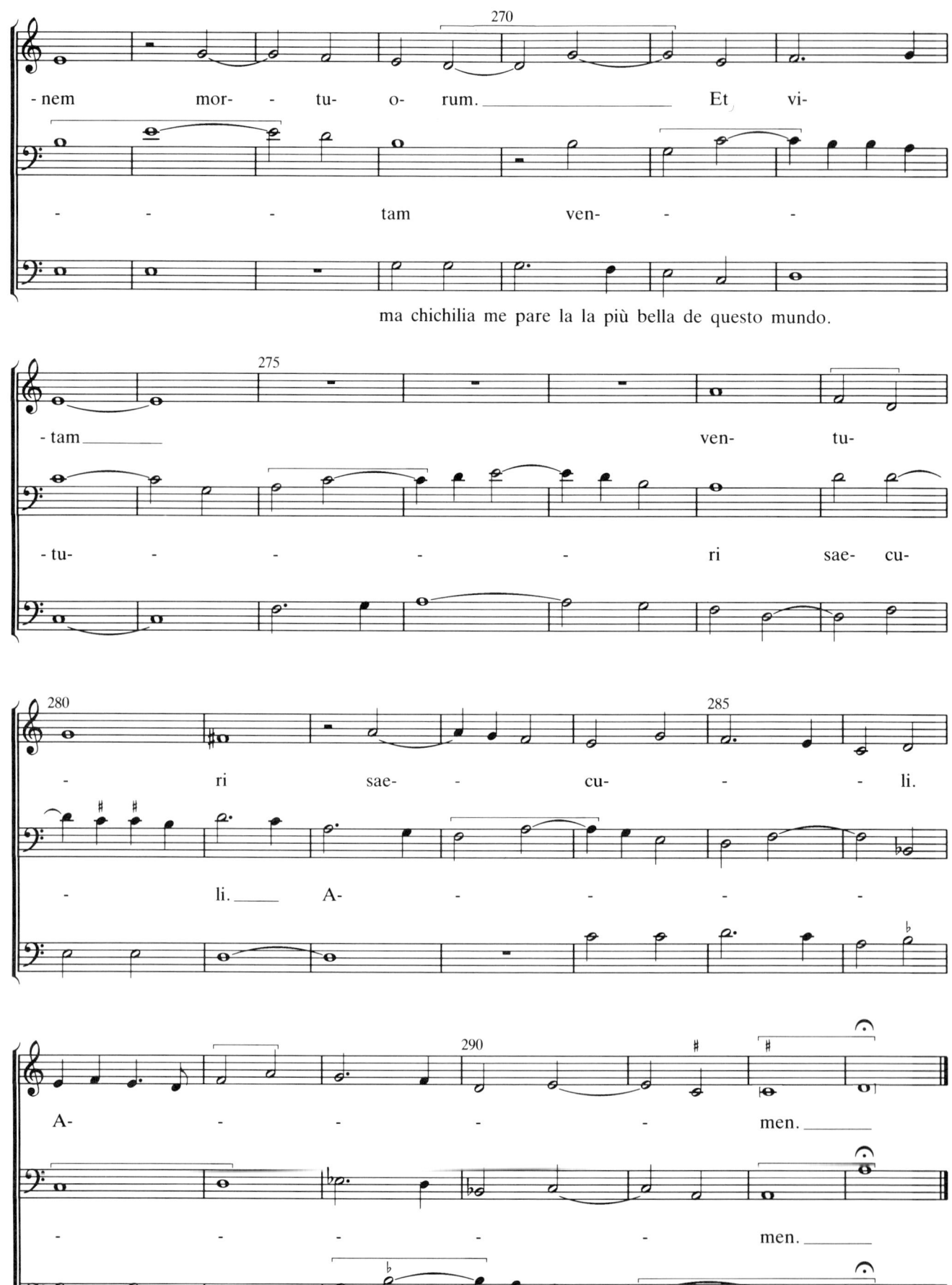

Sanctus

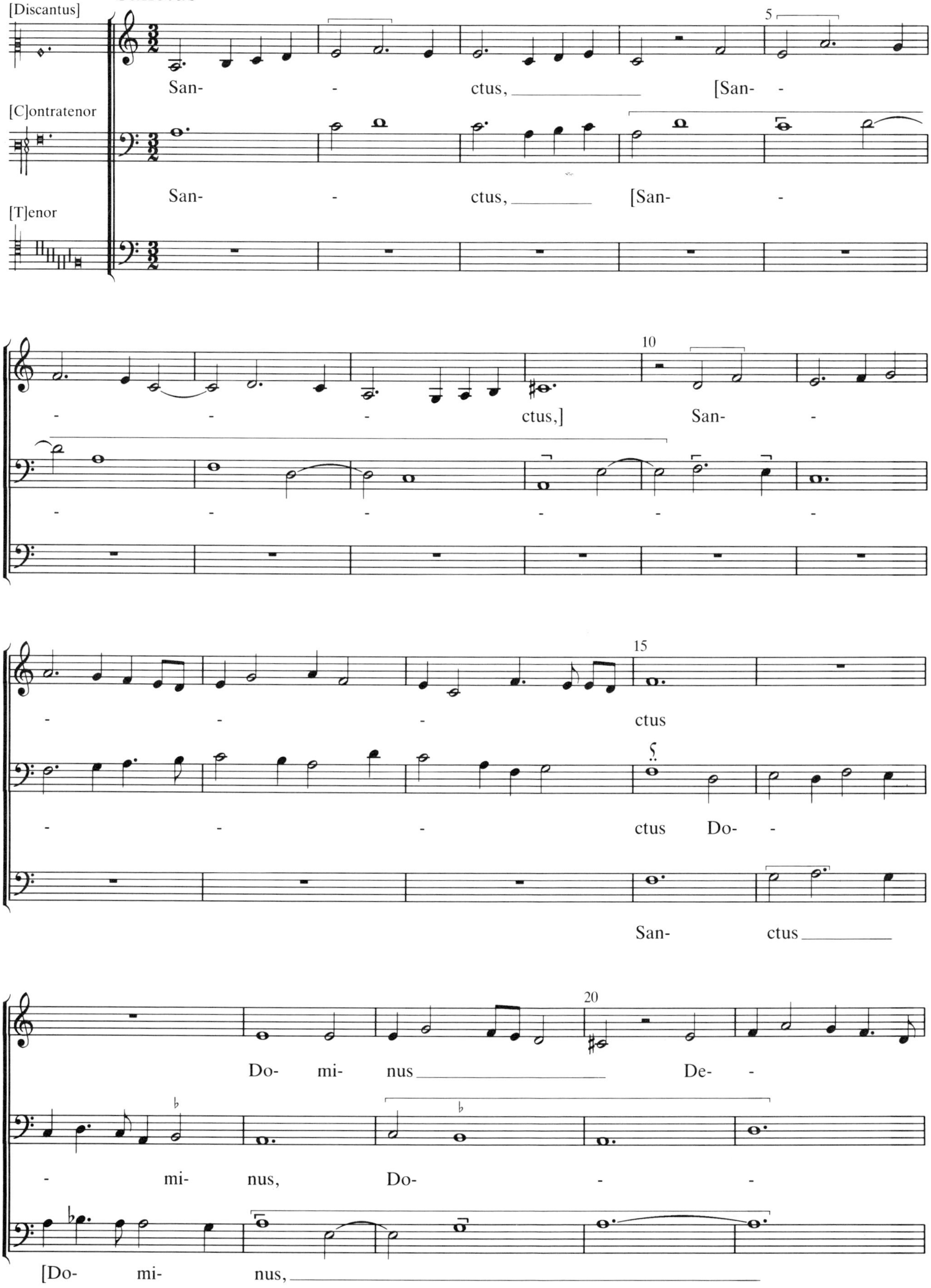
[Discantus]
[C]ontratenor
[T]enor
San- - ctus, [San- -
San- - ctus, [San- -
- - - ctus,] San- -
- - - - - -
- - - ctus
- - - ctus Do- -
San- ctus
Do- mi- nus De- -
- mi- nus, Do- - -
[Do- mi- nus,

Patres nostri peccaverunt

¿Donde estas que non te veo?

Gentil dama non se gana

41

D.C. al Fine

- ran-do vues-tra bel- - dat.
- tan-do vues-tra bon- - - - dat.

Moro perche non day fede

[Discantus]: Mo- ro per- chè non day fe - de Al- la pe- na che m'a- co- - ra. Io te de- man- do,

Tenor: Moro perchè non day fede

Contratenor: Moro perchè non day fede

Morte o merce

Non gusto del male estranio

Porque mas sin duda creas

47

Pues que Dios te fizo tal

¿Qu'es mi vida preguntays?

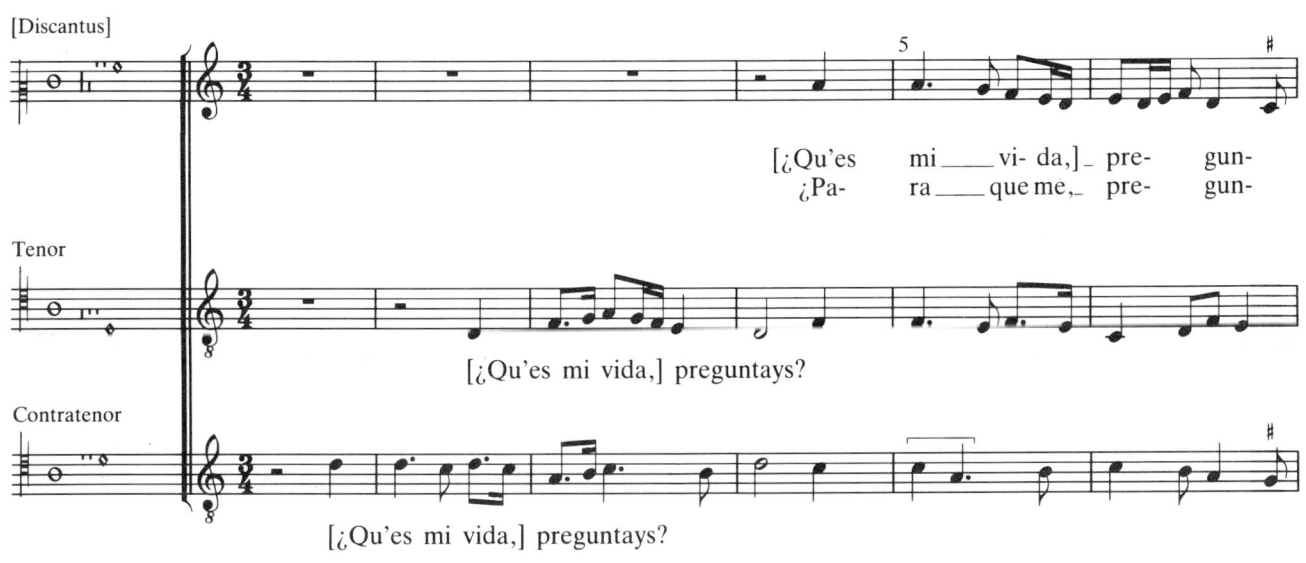

Segun las penas me days

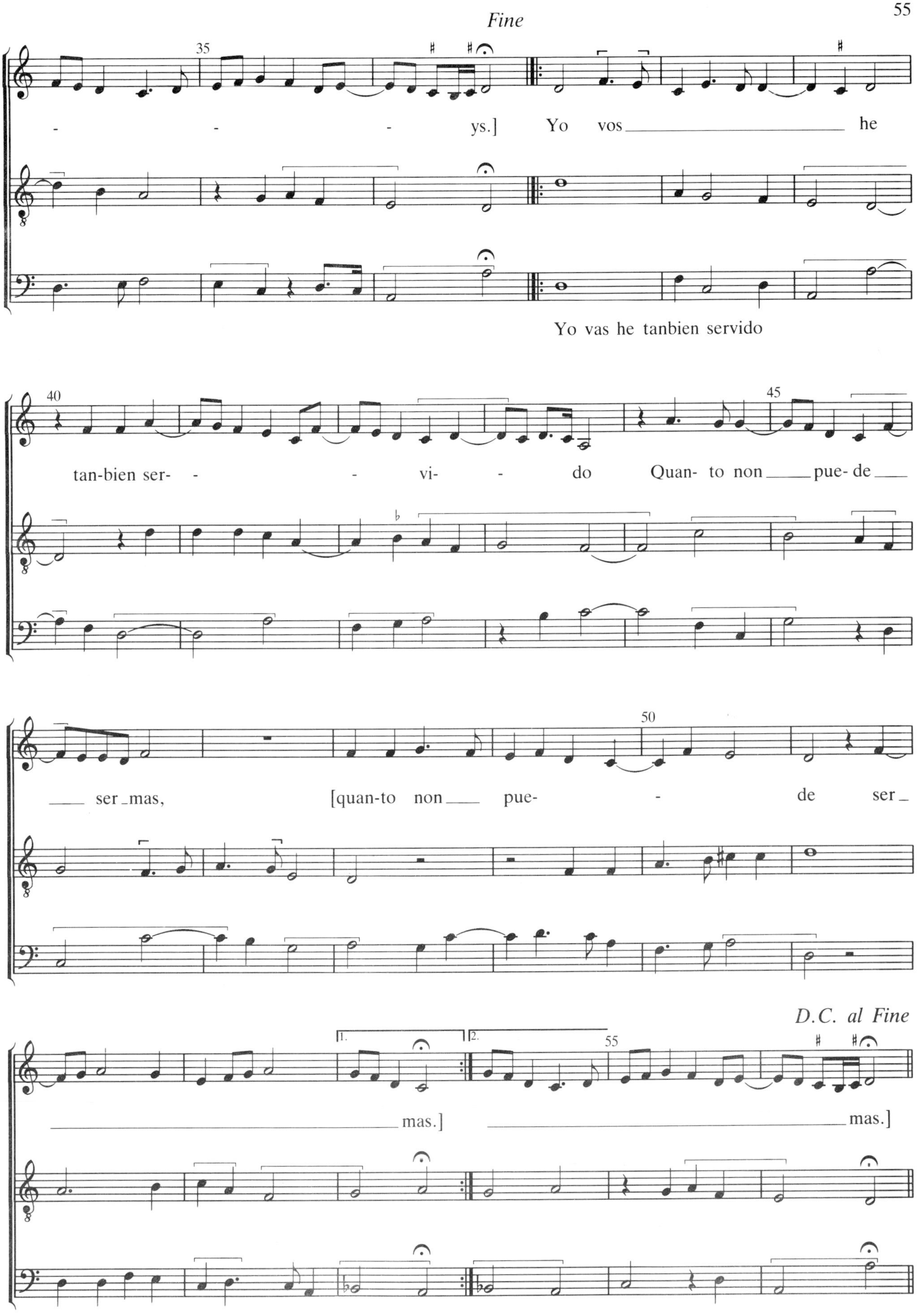
Fine
35
- - - ys.] Yo vos he
Yo vas he tanbien servido
40
45
tan-bien ser- - - vi- - do Quan- to non pue- de
50
ser mas, [quan-to non pue- - de ser
D.C. al Fine
1.
2.
55
mas.] mas.]

Yerra con poco saber

APPENDIX:
Alternate Versions and Double Attributions

Gentil dama non se gana

Morthe merce

Pues que Dios te fiso tal

Pues que Dios te fiso tal: Graçiosa,
Pues que ansi nasçiste tal, En es-

Pues que Dios te fiso tal

[Cornago]

¿Qu'es mi vida preguntays?

Cornago-Ockeghem

Señora, qual soy venido

Cornago-Triana

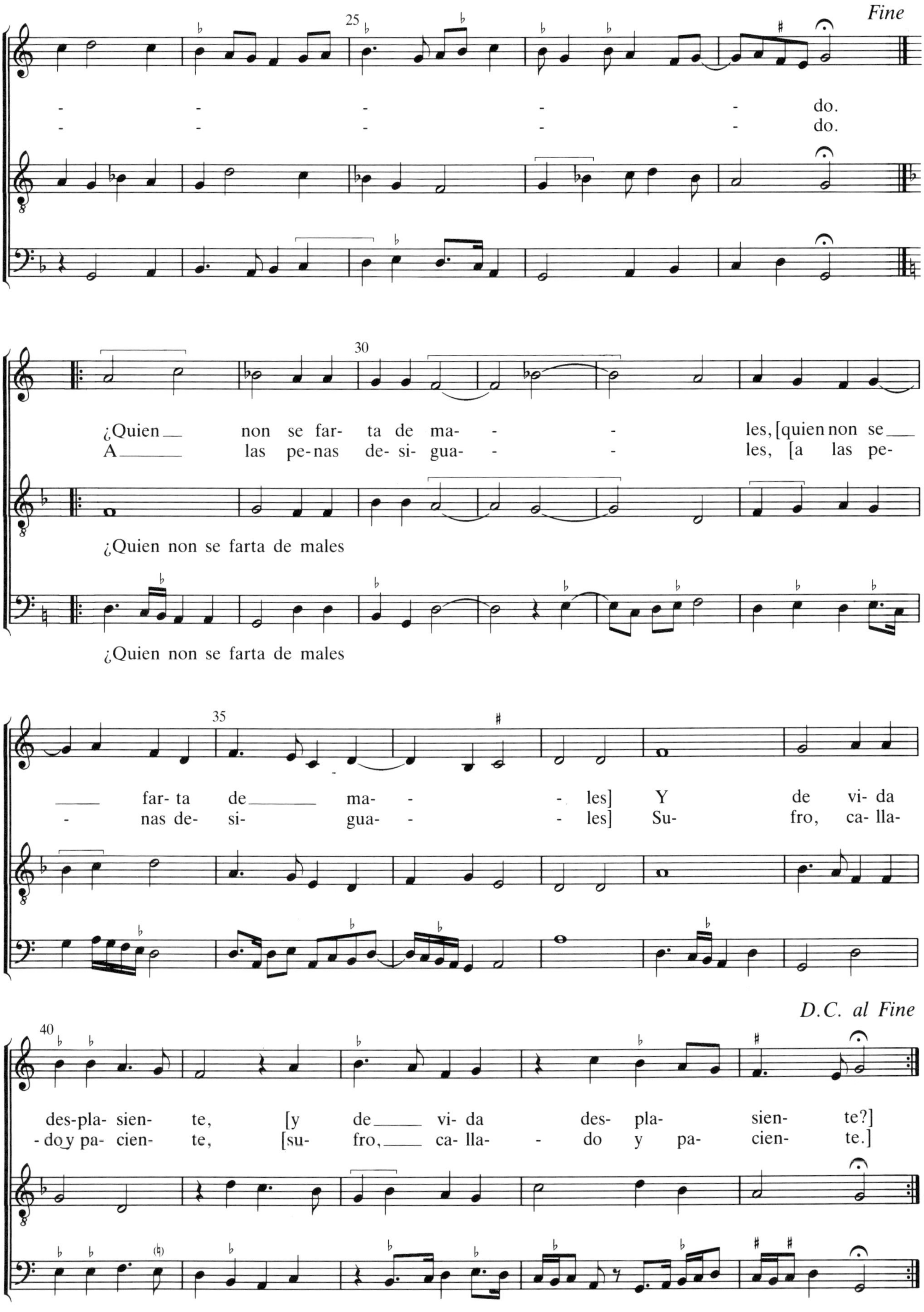
Fine
do.
do.
¿Quien non se far- ta de ma- les, [quien non se far- ta de ma- les]
A las pe-nas de- si- gua- les, [a las pe- nas de- si- gua- les]
¿Quien non se farta de males
¿Quien non se farta de males
Y de vi- da des-pla- sien- te, [y de vi- da des- pla- sien- te?]
Su- fro, ca- lla- -do y pa- cien- te, [su- fro, ca- lla- do y pa- cien- te.]
D.C. al Fine